OFFICIAL
Instant Pot
BOOK

The "I LOVE MY INSTANT POT®"

5-Ingredient

Recipe Book

From *Pot Roast, Potatoes, and Gravy* to *Simple Lemon Cheesecake*, 175 Quick and Easy Recipes

Michelle Fagone of CavegirlCuisine.com

Author of The *"I Love My Instant Pot®" Recipe Book*

Adams Media

New York London Toronto Sydney New Delhi

Dedication

To my best friends, Laura and Cathy:

Thank you for being the best friends any girl could ask for the past 25+ years. Y'all are such amazing examples to follow—as a mom, as a friend, as a woman...as my sister.

Much love, Michelle

Adams Media
An Imprint of Simon & Schuster, Inc.
57 Littlefield Street
Avon, Massachusetts 02322

First Adams Media trade paperback edition February 2021

ADAMS MEDIA and colophon are trademarks of Simon & Schuster.

For information about special discounts for bulk purchases, please contact Simon & Schuster Special Sales at 1-866-506-1949 or business@simonandschuster.com.

The Simon & Schuster Speakers Bureau can bring authors to your live event. For more information or to book an event contact the Simon & Schuster Speakers Bureau at 1-866-248-3049 or visit our website at www.simonspeakers.com.

Photographs by James Stefiuk

Manufactured in the United States of America

1 2020

Library of Congress Cataloging-in-Publication Data has been applied for.

ISBN 978-1-5072-1565-4
ISBN 978-1-5072-1566-1 (ebook)

Contents

Introduction

Life is sometimes hectic, and often the last thing you want to do is run out to a store to buy ingredients to make dinner. If, like most people, you just want a quick, inexpensive, nutritious meal, without the hassle of searching specialty stores for pricey ingredients, then this is your cookbook. Inside you will find delicious and nutritious recipes that all use only five or fewer main ingredients, and to make things even easier they all cook in your Instant Pot®, the time-saving device that allows you to cook a meal and still enjoy life!

Cooking with an Instant Pot® is a life-changing experience. This multifunction cooking tool allows you to sauté, brown, steam, and warm your food. It cooks soups, eggs, and even cheesecakes! And the high-pressure cooking and steaming ability of an Instant Pot® does wonders for steaks, pork shoulders, and chicken. With the touch of a button you'll be able to cook cuts of meat that would normally take hours in just minutes. The Instant Pot® cooks food at a low temperature, but it does it more efficiently than other slow-cooking methods or appliances because it also uses pressure and steam. It is like a pressure cooker and a slow cooker rolled into one. This cooking method also seals in essential vitamins and minerals and allows the Instant Pot® to turn out healthier, better-tasting food that is perfect for when you're on the go.

Whether you've just bought your Instant Pot® or have been using it for years and just need some inspiration, this book is for you. There are 175 delicious and limited-ingredient recipes ranging from Sausage and Sweet Potato Hash and Confetti Quinoa to Cajun Boiled Peanuts and Banana Bread Pudding. The more you cook and experiment, the more you'll realize how versatile the Instant Pot® really is—whether you are making a hearty breakfast, a main dish, or a decadent dessert. So plug in your Instant Pot® and get ready to enjoy some amazing, delicious, and quick and easy meals.

Cooking with an Instant Pot®

So you're about to venture into the amazing world of Instant Pot® cooking...but you're not sure where or how to start. Don't worry; this chapter will give you the information you need to get started. Here you'll learn what all those buttons on your Instant Pot® do, how to release the pressure from the Instant Pot® when the cooking time is up, how to keep your Instant Pot® clean, and more.

Even though you'll learn all this information in this chapter, it's important that you read the owner's manual as well. That user manual is your key to successfully creating the recipes throughout this book. In addition to pointing out the basic functions of the appliance, it will tell you how to do an initial test run using water to get familiar with the Instant Pot®. I can't stress enough that you need to do this. It will both familiarize you with the appliance and take away some of your anxiety. In addition, this first run will help steam clean your pot before you use it to make your favorite recipe.

But for now, let's take a look at some Instant Pot® basics.

Function Buttons

You are staring at the Instant Pot®, and there are so many buttons. Which one should you use? Most of the function buttons seem obvious, but it is important to note that several are set with preprogrammed default cooking times. Also, keep in mind that every button option on the Instant Pot® is programmed with a 10-second delay, meaning that cooking begins 10 seconds after you hit the button. Most likely you will use the Manual or Pressure Cook button the most because you will have more control, but read on for more detailed information regarding the remaining function buttons.

Manual or Pressure Cook button. Depending on the model of Instant Pot®, there is a button labeled either Manual or Pressure Cook. This might be the most-used button on the Instant Pot®. The default pressure setting is High; however, you can toggle the pressure from High to Low by pressing the Pressure button. Use the Plus and Minus buttons to adjust the pressurized cooking time.

Sauté button. This button helps the Instant Pot® act as a skillet for sautéing vegetables or searing meat prior to adding the remaining ingredients of a recipe, and it is used for simmering sauces as well. There are three temperature settings—Normal, Less, and More—that can be accessed using the Adjust button. The Normal setting is for sautéing, the Less setting is for simmering, and the More setting is for searing meat.

Keep the lid open when using the Sauté button to avoid pressure building up.

Soup button. This button is used to cook soups and broths at high pressure for a default of 30 minutes. The Adjust button allows you to change the cooking time to 20 or 40 minutes.

Porridge button. This button is used to cook porridge, congee, and jook in the Instant Pot® at high pressure for a default of 20 minutes. The Adjust button allows you to change the cooking time to 15 or 40 minutes.

Poultry button. This button is used to cook chicken, turkey, and even duck at high pressure for a default of 15 minutes. The Adjust button allows you to change the cooking time to 5 or 30 minutes.

Meat/Stew button. This button is used to cook red meats and stew meats at high pressure for a default of 35 minutes. The Adjust button allows you to change the cooking time to 20 or 45 minutes.

Bean/Chili button. This button is used to cook dried beans and chili at high pressure for a default of 30 minutes. The Adjust button allows you to change the cooking time to 25 or 40 minutes.

Rice button. This button is used to cook white rice such as jasmine or basmati at low pressure. The Instant Pot® will automatically set the default cooking time by sensing the amount of water and rice in the cooking vessel.

Multigrain button. This button is used to cook grains such as wild rice, quinoa, and barley at high pressure for a default of

40 minutes. The Adjust button allows you to change the cooking time to 20 or 60 minutes.

Steam button. This button is excellent for steaming vegetables and seafood using your steamer basket. It steams for a default of 10 minutes. The Adjust button allows you to change the cooking time to 3 or 15 minutes. Quick-release the steam immediately after the timer beeps to avoid overcooking the food.

Slow Cook button. This button allows the Instant Pot® to cook like a slow cooker. It defaults to a 4-hour cook time. The Adjust button allows you to change the temperature to Less, Normal, or More, which correspond to a slow cooker's Low, Normal, or High. The Plus and Minus buttons allow you to adjust the cooking time.

Keep Warm/Cancel button. When the Instant Pot® is being programmed or in operation, pressing this button cancels the operation and returns the Instant Pot® to a standby state. When the Instant Pot® is in the standby state, pressing this button again activates the Keep Warm function.

Automatic Keep Warm function. After the ingredients in the Instant Pot® are finished cooking, the pot automatically switches over to the Keep Warm function and will keep your food warm up to 10 hours. This is perfect for large cuts of meat as well as for soups, stews, and chili, allowing the spices and flavors to really marry for an even better taste. The first digit on the LED display will show an "L" to indicate that the Instant Pot® is in the Keep Warm cycle, and the clock will count up from 0 seconds to 10 hours.

Timer button. This button allows you to delay the start of cooking up to 24 hours. After you select a cooking program and make any time adjustments, press the Timer button and use the Plus or Minus buttons to enter the delayed hours; press the Timer button again and use the Plus or Minus buttons to enter the delayed minutes. You can press the Keep Warm/Cancel button to cancel the timed delay. The Timer function doesn't work with Sauté, Yogurt, or Keep Warm functions.

How Does Food Cook in 0 Minutes?

If you are confused about how some recipes require 0 minutes to cook, it's not a typo. Some vegetables and seafoods that require only minimal steaming are set at zero cooking time. Food can actually be cooked in the time that it takes the Instant Pot® to achieve pressure.

Locking and Pressure-Release Methods

Other than the Sauté function, where the lid should be off, and the Slow Cook and Keep Warm functions, where the lid can be on or off, most of the cooking you'll do in the Instant Pot® will be under pressure, which means you need to know how to lock the lid before pressurized cooking and how to safely release the pressure after cooking. Once your ingredients are in the inner pot of the Instant Pot®, lock the lid by putting it on the Instant Pot® with the triangle mark aligned with the Unlocked

mark on the rim of the Instant Pot®. Then turn the lid 30 degrees clockwise until the triangle mark on the lid is aligned with the Locked mark on the rim. Turn the pointed end of the pressure-release handle on top of the lid to the Sealing position. After your cooking program has ended or you've pressed the Keep Warm/Cancel button to end the cooking, there are two ways you can release the pressure:

Natural-release method. To naturally release the pressure, simply wait until the Instant Pot® has cooled sufficiently for all the pressure to be released and the float valve to drop, normally about 10–15 minutes. You can either unplug the Instant Pot® while the pressure releases naturally or let the pressure release while it is still on the Keep Warm function.

Quick-release method. The quick-release method stifles the cooking process and helps unlock the lid for immediate serving. To quickly release the pressure on the Instant Pot®, make sure you are wearing oven mitts, then turn the pressure-release handle to the Venting position to let out steam until the float valve drops. This is generally not recommended for starchy items or large volumes of liquid (e.g., soup) so as to avoid any splattering that may occur. Be prepared, because the noise and geyser effect of the releasing steam during the quick-release method can be off-putting. Also, if you own dogs, this release is apparently the most frightening part of their day, so take caution.

Pot-in-Pot Accessories

Pot-in-pot cooking is when you place another cooking dish inside the Instant Pot® for a particular recipe. The Instant Pot® is straightforward and comes with an inner pot and steam rack; however, there are many other recipes that can be made with the purchase of a few other accessories, including a springform pan, cake pan, glass bowl, and ramekins. Also available online are multiple accessory packages to fit all of your needs.

7" springform pan. A 7" springform pan is the perfect size for making a cheesecake and many other desserts in an Instant Pot®. It is the right dimension to fit inside the pot, and it makes a dessert for four to six people.

6" cake pan. A 6" pan is excellent for making a small cake in the Instant Pot®. It can serve four to six people depending on the serving size. This pan is perfect for a family craving a small dessert without committing to leftovers.

7-cup glass baking dish. A 7-cup bowl fits perfectly in the Instant Pot® and works great for eggs and bread puddings that generally would burn on the bottom of the pot insert. The items in the bowl sit up on the inserted steam rack and are cooked with the steam and pressure of the pot.

Ramekins. These baking dishes usually come in 4-ounce sizes and are the perfect vessels for tasty individual custards.

Steamer basket. A steamer basket helps create a raised shelf for steaming. Shop around, as there are several variations, including metal and silicone steamer baskets. Some even have handles to make it easier to remove them after the cooking process.

Silicone egg mold with lid. This is a multi-use silicone pan made by Instant Pot® with seven separate cups perfect for egg bites, muffins, cupcakes, baby food, yogurt, and ice cream.

Silicone baking cupcake liners. Silicone baking cups are great for mini meatloaves, cupcakes, on-the-go frittatas, and little quick breads.

Although these accessories can help you branch out and make different recipes with the Instant Pot®, there are many recipes you can make using just the inner pot and steam rack that come with your appliance. These are just handy items you can purchase along the way to use with what will soon become your favorite heat source in the kitchen.

Accessory Removal

Cooking pot-in-pot is a great idea until it's time to remove the inserted cooking dish. Because of the tight space, it is almost impossible to use thick oven mitts to reach down and grip something evenly without tipping one side of the cooking vessel and spilling the cooked item. There are a few ways around this:

Retriever tongs. Retriever tongs are a helpful tool for removing hot bowls and pans from the Instant Pot®.

Mini mitts. Small oven mitts are helpful when lifting pots out of an Instant Pot® after the cooking process, especially the type made of silicone. They are more heat-resistant and less cumbersome than traditional oven mitts, which can prove to be bulky in the tight space of the cooker.

Aluminum foil sling. This is a quick, inexpensive fix to the problem of lifting a heated dish out of an Instant Pot®. Take a 10″ × 10″ square of aluminum foil and fold it back and forth until you have a 2″ × 10″ sling. Place this sling underneath the bowl or pan before cooking so that you can easily lift up the heated dish.

Although necessary if you do pot-in-pot cooking, these retrieval tools are not needed if you are simply using the interior pot that comes with the appliance upon purchase. A slotted spoon will do the trick for most other meals.

Cleaning Your Instant Pot®

When cleaning up after using your Instant Pot®, the first thing you should do is unplug it and let it cool down. Then you can break down the following parts to clean and inspect for any trapped food particles:

Inner pot. The inner pot, the cooking vessel, is dishwasher safe; however, the high heat causes rainbowing, or discoloration, on stainless steel. To avoid this, hand-wash the pot.

Outer heating unit. Wipe the interior and exterior with a damp cloth. Do not submerge in water, as it is an electrical appliance.

Steam rack. The steam rack is dishwasher safe or can be cleaned with soap and water.

Lid. The lid needs to be broken down into individual parts before washing. The sealing ring, the float valve, the pressure-release handle, and the anti-block shield all need to be cleaned in different ways:

Sealing ring. Once this ring is removed, check the integrity of the silicone. If it is torn or cracked, it will not seal properly and may hinder the cooking process, in which case it should not be used. The sealing ring needs to be removed and washed each time because the ring has a tendency to hold odors when cooking. Vinegar or lemon juice are excellent for reducing odors. You can purchase additional rings for a nominal price. Many Instant Pot® users buy more than one ring and use one for meats and a separate one for desserts and milder dishes.

Float valve. The float valve is a safety feature that serves as a latch lock that prevents the lid from being opened during the cooking process. Make sure this valve can move easily and is not obstructed by any food particles.

Pressure-release handle. This is the venting handle on top of the lid. It can be pulled out for cleaning. It should be loose, so don't worry. This allows it to move when necessary.

Anti-block shield. The anti-block shield is the little silver "basket" underneath the lid. It is located directly below the vent. This shield can and should be removed and cleaned. It blocks any foods, especially starches, so they don't clog the vent.

So, now that you know about all the safety features, buttons, and parts of the Instant Pot® and know how to clean everything, it's time for the fun part. The cooking process is where the excitement begins. From breakfast to dessert and everything in between, *The "I Love My Instant Pot®" 5-Ingredient Recipe Book* has you covered.

Pantry Staples

Each recipe in this book has five or fewer main ingredients, but also included are some kitchen pantry staples in addition to those five to ensure the tastes and textures of your meals come out perfect. Following are twelve staples that, if you have them on hand, should help you maneuver through this cookbook with ease of ingredients.

- All-purpose flour
- Baking powder
- Baking soda
- Broth
- Garlic salt
- Granulated sugar
- Ground black pepper
- Hot sauce
- Italian seasoning
- Olive oil
- Salt
- Vanilla extract

These items were chosen for their stability and versatility.

For the broth, please note that there are recipes that require beef, chicken, or vegetable broth. These are all shelf-stable items, unless freshly made, that can be stored in the pantry. Most broths, although flavors will vary, can be subbed for other broths. For example, if you prefer vegetable broth, use this. Remember that each recipe is ultimately yours, and the recipes in this book are only a guide to your creations.

2

Breakfast

Mornings seem to be the busiest time of day for most. Whether you are a parent rushing the family to the car, a student scurrying to class, or just not a morning person, the Instant Pot® can help you get that best meal of the day in your belly with little fuss. It offers shortened cooking time, and it saves you from having to stand over a skillet; all you have to do is add the ingredients, press a button, and go get ready to tackle your day.

From eggs to doughnut holes, this chapter has got you covered with a myriad of delicious breakfast recipes, including Pimiento Cheese Grits, Nutty Steel-Cut Oats, and Cinnamon Roll Doughnut Holes. And once you get comfortable with some of the basics, you should feel free to get creative and make some of your own morning masterpieces.

Hard-"Boiled" Eggs

A 6-minute cook time will yield hard egg whites and firm yolks. You may want to add or subtract a minute to your cooking time if you like them cooked more or less. Once you find your sweet spot, this is the easiest way to hard-"boil" your eggs!

Pantry Staples: none
Hands-On Time: 5 minutes
Cook Time: 6 minutes

Serves 6

1 cup water
6 large eggs

JAMMY EGGS!

If you like a softer center to your eggs, decrease your cooking time to 3 minutes on high pressure. Jammy eggs are the best of both worlds. The white is set and somewhat firm, and the center is almost spreadable...not super runny and not hard-boiled, but like the consistency of jam. Get it? And a side note—if you like to take photos of your food, this is the egg for your *Instagram* account!

1 Add water to the Instant Pot® and insert steamer basket. Place eggs in basket. Lock lid.

2 Press the Manual or Pressure Cook button and adjust time to 6 minutes. When timer beeps, quick-release pressure until float valve drops. Unlock lid.

3 Create an ice bath by adding 1 cup ice and 1 cup water to a medium bowl. Transfer eggs to ice bath to stop the cooking process.

4 Peel eggs. Slice each egg directly onto a plate. Serve immediately.

PER SERVING:

CALORIES: 77 | FAT: 4g | PROTEIN: 6g | SODIUM: 62mg | FIBER: 0g | CARBOHYDRATES: 1g | NET CARBS: 1g | SUGAR: 1g

Lemony Pancake Bites with Blueberry Syrup

Lemon and blueberries are such a sophisticated combination, but this recipe couldn't be any easier to make. You can also change up the combination by subbing out the lemon for orange and the blueberry syrup for strawberry syrup!

Pantry Staples: salt
Hands-On Time: 10 minutes
Cook Time: 24 minutes

Serves 4

1 (7-ounce) packet Hungry Jack buttermilk pancake mix
⅔ cup whole milk
Juice and zest of ½ medium lemon
⅛ teaspoon salt
1 cup water
½ cup blueberry syrup

1 Grease a seven-hole silicone egg mold.

2 In a medium bowl, combine pancake mix, milk, lemon juice and zest, and salt. Fill egg mold with half of batter.

3 Add water to the Instant Pot® and insert steam rack. Place filled egg mold on steam rack. Lock lid.

4 Press the Manual or Pressure Cook button and adjust time to 12 minutes. When timer beeps, quick-release pressure until float valve drops. Unlock lid.

5 Allow pancake bites to cool, about 3 minutes until cool enough to handle. Pop out of mold. Repeat with remaining batter.

6 Serve warm with syrup for dipping.

PER SERVING:

CALORIES: 117 | FAT: 2g | PROTEIN: 6g | SODIUM: 562mg | FIBER: 0g | CARBOHYDRATES: 62g | NET CARBS: 62g | SUGAR: 19g

Tomato Mozzarella Basil Egg Bites

The Italian trinity...or at least it should be. Tomatoes, mozzarella, and basil just feel like they were meant to be eaten together, and these egg bites are no exception. These savory and delicious treats require only a few ingredients and will help you start your day with a smile on your face!

Pantry Staples: salt, ground black pepper
Hands-On Time: 10 minutes
Cook Time: 8 minutes

Serves 6

4 large eggs
2 tablespoons grated yellow onion
½ teaspoon salt
½ teaspoon ground black pepper
6 cherry tomatoes, quartered
¼ cup grated mozzarella cheese
2 tablespoons chopped fresh basil
1 cup water

1 Grease six silicone cupcake liners.

2 In a medium bowl, whisk together eggs, onion, salt, and pepper. Distribute egg mixture evenly among cupcake liners. Add tomatoes, cheese, and basil to each cup.

3 Add water to the Instant Pot® and insert steam rack. Place steamer basket on steam rack. Carefully place cupcake liners in basket. Lock lid.

4 Press the Manual or Pressure Cook button and adjust time to 8 minutes. When timer beeps, quick-release pressure until float valve drops. Unlock lid.

5 Remove egg bites. Serve warm.

PER SERVING:

CALORIES: 63 | FAT: 4g | PROTEIN: 5g | SODIUM: 266mg | FIBER: 0g | CARBOHYDRATES: 5g | NET CARBS: 5g | SUGAR: 1g

CAN I FREEZE EGG BITES?

Yes! That makes these a great item to put on your prep day list. Once the egg bites have completely cooled, simply put them in an airtight freezer-safe container and freeze up to 4 weeks. This will save you money, time, and calories by skipping the drive-through on busy mornings. Either microwave your egg bite, or put it in the refrigerator the night before and then simply reheat it in your oven or toaster oven.

Bacon Cheddar Scrambled Egg Muffins

These egg muffins are great for breakfast on the go. Whether you make these the night before and microwave them the next morning or just cook them before you head out, these classic flavors make for the happiest of mornings!

Pantry Staples: salt, ground black pepper
Hands-On Time: 10 minutes
Cook Time: 8 minutes

Serves 6

4 large eggs
2 tablespoons whole milk
2 tablespoons grated yellow onion
½ teaspoon salt
½ teaspoon ground black pepper
5 slices bacon, cooked and crumbled
¼ cup grated Cheddar cheese
1 cup water

---

1 Grease six silicone cupcake liners.

2 In a medium bowl, whisk together eggs, milk, onion, salt, and pepper. Distribute egg mixture evenly among cupcake liners. Add equal amounts of bacon and cheese to each cup.

3 Add water to the Instant Pot® and insert steam rack. Place steamer basket on steam rack. Carefully place muffin cups in basket. Lock lid.

4 Press the Manual or Pressure Cook button and adjust time to 8 minutes. When timer beeps, quick-release pressure until float valve drops. Unlock lid.

5 Remove egg muffins. Serve warm.

PER SERVING:

CALORIES: 116 | FAT: 7g | PROTEIN: 9g | SODIUM: 434mg | FIBER: 0g | CARBOHYDRATES: 1g | NET CARBS: 1g | SUGAR: 1g

Pimiento Cheese Grits

The Instant Pot® takes all the labor and guesswork out of making grits! These cheesy grits are taken up a notch by the simple addition of pimientos. These heart-shaped, very mild, and sweet peppers add another layer of flavor to your grits. Add a biscuit to your plate and sop up all of that goodness!

Pantry Staples: salt, ground black pepper
Hands-On Time: 5 minutes
Cook Time: 10 minutes

Serves 4

¾ cup plus 1½ cups water, divided
1 cup stone-ground grits
2 tablespoons unsalted butter
1 teaspoon salt
½ teaspoon ground black pepper
½ cup grated sharp Cheddar cheese
1 (4-ounce) jar diced pimientos, drained

1. Add ¾ cup water to the Instant Pot® and insert steam rack.

2. In a 7-cup glass baking dish that fits down into the pot insert, combine grits, butter, remaining 1½ cups water, salt, and pepper. Lock lid.

3. Press the Rice button. (The Instant Pot® will determine the cooking time, about 10 minutes pressurized cooking time.) When timer beeps, quick-release pressure until float valve drops. Unlock lid.

4. Stir in cheese and pimientos. Serve warm.

PER SERVING:

CALORIES: 258 | FAT: 10g | PROTEIN: 7g | SODIUM: 676mg | FIBER: 2g | CARBOHYDRATES: 32g | NET CARBS: 30g | SUGAR: 1g

UNSALTED VERSUS SALTED BUTTER

The main reason for using unsalted butter in recipes is because you can control the amount of salt that is included. This is especially true for when butter is used in baking when precise measurements are required. But, as far as butter smeared on a biscuit or piece of toast? Salted butter is always the answer!

Sausage and Sweet Potato Hash

The Instant Pot® is the perfect vessel for creating a yummy hash. Achieving those soft potatoes is difficult in a skillet unless you steam the potatoes beforehand. This recipe is a must-make. Don't forget to serve a poached or over-easy egg over the top!

Pantry Staples: Italian seasoning, salt, ground black pepper
Hands-On Time: 10 minutes
Cook Time: 10 minutes

Serves 4

½ pound ground pork sausage
1 large sweet potato, peeled and grated
1 small yellow onion, peeled and diced
2 cloves garlic, peeled and minced
1 medium green bell pepper, seeded and diced
1 tablespoon Italian seasoning
½ teaspoon salt
½ teaspoon ground black pepper
2 cups water

1 Press the Sauté button on the Instant Pot®. Stir-fry sausage, sweet potato, onion, garlic, bell pepper, Italian seasoning, salt, and black pepper 3–5 minutes until onions are translucent. Press the Cancel button.

2 Transfer mixture to a greased 7-cup glass baking dish.

3 Add water to the Instant Pot® and insert steam rack. Place dish on steam rack. Lock lid.

4 Press the Manual or Pressure Cook button and adjust time to 5 minutes. When timer beeps, quick-release pressure until float valve drops. Unlock lid.

5 Remove dish from the Instant Pot®. Spoon hash onto plates and serve.

PER SERVING:

CALORIES: 251 | FAT: 17g | PROTEIN: 10g | SODIUM: 722mg | FIBER: 2g | CARBOHYDRATES: 13g | NET CARBS: 11g | SUGAR: 4g

INGREDIENT SUBSTITUTIONS

The excellent thing about this recipe is that you can substitute ingredients with what you already have in your kitchen. Use white potatoes instead of sweet potatoes. Use bacon instead of sausage. Use a jalapeño instead of the bell pepper. Have some fresh herbs on hand? Throw them in!

Grandma's Country Gravy

Although a perfect complement for your morning biscuits, this versatile sauce will also make your mashed potatoes, pork chops, or chicken-fried steak sing a song. Creamy and peppery, you'll want to double your batch and refrigerate. Just add a little water while reheating to loosen it up the next day.

Pantry Staples: chicken broth, all-purpose flour, salt, ground black pepper
Hands-On Time: 5 minutes
Cook Time: 16 minutes

Serves 6

2 tablespoons unsalted butter
1 pound ground pork sausage
1 small sweet onion, peeled and diced
¼ cup chicken broth
¼ cup all-purpose flour
1½ cups heavy cream
½ teaspoon salt
1 tablespoon ground black pepper

ADD IT IN!
Add a tablespoon of cornmeal when you whisk in your flour and you will change your Country Gravy into Sawmill Gravy! For a deeper and spicier gravy, purchase Italian pork sausage, either mild or spicy.

1 Press the Sauté button on the Instant Pot®. Add butter and heat until melted. Add sausage and onion and stir-fry 3–5 minutes until onions are translucent. The pork will still be a little pink in places. Add broth. Press the Cancel button. Lock lid.

2 Press the Manual or Pressure Cook button and adjust time to 1 minute. When timer beeps, quick-release pressure until float valve drops. Unlock lid. Whisk in flour, cream, salt, and pepper.

3 Press the Keep Warm button and let the gravy sit about 5–10 minutes to allow to thicken. Remove from heat. Serve warm.

PER SERVING:

CALORIES: 442 | FAT: 36g | PROTEIN: 18g | SODIUM: 306mg | FIBER: 1g | CARBOHYDRATES: 9g | NET CARBS: 8g | SUGAR: 3g

Crustless Power Quiche

This dish will help you eat like a champion and feel like a champion. It is packed full of healthy protein from the eggs and sausage and healthy fats from the avocado. With this delicious and nutritious recipe, you'll feel like you'll have the power to take on any day.

Pantry Staples: salt, ground black pepper, olive oil
Hands-On Time: 10 minutes
Cook Time: 9 minutes

Serves 2

6 large eggs
½ teaspoon salt
½ teaspoon ground black pepper
2 teaspoons olive oil
½ cup diced red onion
1 medium red bell pepper, seeded and diced
¼ pound ground pork sausage
1½ cups water
1 medium avocado, peeled, pitted, and diced

1 In a medium bowl, whisk together eggs, salt, and black pepper. Set aside.

2 Press the Sauté button on the Instant Pot® and heat oil. Stir-fry onion, bell pepper, and sausage 3–4 minutes until sausage starts to brown and onions are tender. Press the Cancel button.

3 Transfer sausage mixture to a greased 7-cup glass bowl. Pour whisked eggs over the mixture.

4 Add water to the Instant Pot® and insert steam rack. Place bowl with egg mixture on steam rack. Lock lid.

5 Press the Manual or Pressure Cook button and adjust time to 5 minutes. When timer beeps, quick-release pressure until float valve drops. Unlock lid.

6 Remove bowl from pot. Let sit at room temperature 5–10 minutes to allow the eggs to set, then remove quiche from bowl, slice, and garnish with avocado. Serve warm.

PER SERVING:

CALORIES: 530 | FAT: 36g | PROTEIN: 33g | SODIUM: 840mg | FIBER: 7g | CARBOHYDRATES: 15g | NET CARBS: 8g | SUGAR: 5g

Peanut Butter and Banana Oatmeal

The flavors of peanut butter with banana is a classic combination that pleases eaters of all ages. This quick and easy oatmeal combines those flavors with the warm spice of cinnamon and the sweetness of brown sugar for a breakfast that is sure to get your morning going!

Pantry Staples: vanilla extract, salt
Hands-On Time: 5 minutes
Cook Time: 7 minutes

Serves 2

1 cup old-fashioned oats
1¼ cups water
1 large ripe banana, peeled and mashed
1 tablespoon packed light brown sugar
¼ teaspoon vanilla extract
¼ teaspoon ground cinnamon
⅛ teaspoon salt
2 tablespoons crunchy peanut butter

ADD IT IN!
Try pouring a little milk over your cooked oatmeal for a creamier and looser dish. And if you want some additional crunchy texture, garnish with chopped peanuts.

1 In the Instant Pot®, add oats, water, banana, brown sugar, vanilla, cinnamon, and salt. Stir to combine. Lock lid.

2 Press the Manual or Pressure Cook button and adjust time to 7 minutes. When timer beeps, let pressure release naturally until float valve drops. Unlock lid.

3 Stir in peanut butter, then spoon oatmeal into two bowls. Serve warm.

PER SERVING:

CALORIES: 335 | FAT: 9g | PROTEIN: 10g | SODIUM: 151mg | FIBER: 7g | CARBOHYDRATES: 54g | NET CARBS: 47g | SUGAR: 17g

Pecan Chocolate Chip Breakfast Oats

This quick breakfast is perfect for when you want some good nutrition but you don't want to feel like it's healthy. To make this healthier without sacrificing the delicious taste, make those chocolate chips dark chocolate for a lower sugar rush.

Pantry Staples: vanilla extract, salt
Hands-On Time: 5 minutes
Cook Time: 7 minutes

Serves 2

1 cup old-fashioned oats
1 cup water
1 cup whole milk
¼ teaspoon vanilla extract
2 tablespoons packed light brown sugar
2 tablespoons chopped pecans
⅛ teaspoon salt
2 tablespoons mini chocolate chips

1 In the Instant Pot®, add oats, water, milk, vanilla, brown sugar, pecans, and salt. Stir to combine. Lock lid.

2 Press the Manual or Pressure Cook button and adjust time to 7 minutes. When timer beeps, quick-release pressure until float valve drops. Unlock lid.

3 Stir oatmeal, then spoon into two bowls and garnish with chocolate chips. Serve warm.

PER SERVING:

CALORIES: 383 | FAT: 13g | PROTEIN: 11g | SODIUM: 210mg | FIBER: 5g | CARBOHYDRATES: 54g | NET CARBS: 49g | SUGAR: 26g

CHOCOLATE CHIP SUBSTITUTIONS

Not only are there dark, milk, and white chocolate chips available, but there are also numerous other flavor choices in chips: toffee, peanut butter, mint, and butterscotch, to name a few. Browse the baking aisle the next time you are at your local grocery store. You may be surprised at your options!

Nutty Steel-Cut Oats

A healthy grain, steel-cut oats are lower on the glycemic index than their "regular" counterpart. Steel-cut oats are minimally processed and have a higher fiber content. These plant-based proteins are high in vitamins, minerals, and antioxidants. And, the Instant Pot® does them justice while you go about your morning routine.

Pantry Staples: vanilla extract, salt
Hands-On Time: 5 minutes
Cook Time: 12 minutes

Serves 2

1½ cups steel-cut oats
2 cups water
1 cup whole milk
½ teaspoon vanilla extract
2 tablespoons packed light brown sugar
2 tablespoons chopped walnuts
⅛ teaspoon salt

1 In the Instant Pot®, add oats, water, milk, vanilla, brown sugar, walnuts, and salt. Stir to combine. Lock lid.

2 Press the Manual or Pressure Cook button and adjust time to 12 minutes. When timer beeps, quick-release pressure until float valve drops. Unlock lid.

3 Stir oatmeal, then spoon into two bowls. Serve warm.

PER SERVING:

CALORIES: 343 | FAT: 9g | PROTEIN: 13g | SODIUM: 100mg | FIBER: 8g | CARBOHYDRATES: 54g | NET CARBS: 46g | SUGAR: 10g

Bacon Onion Cheddar Frittata

There is something so simple and delicious about the morning flavors of eggs, bacon, and cheese. Those few ingredients make a powerhouse meal that will satisfy you and keep you feeling full all morning long. This quick frittata could serve just two as a meal or serve four guests with the addition of some fresh fruit or even a salad for a nice brunch.

Pantry Staples: Italian seasoning, salt, ground black pepper, olive oil
Hands-On Time: 10 minutes
Cook Time: 12 minutes

Serves 4

6 large eggs
2 teaspoons Italian seasoning
½ cup shredded Cheddar cheese
½ teaspoon salt
¼ teaspoon ground black pepper
1 tablespoon olive oil
4 slices bacon, diced
1 small yellow onion, peeled and diced
1 cup water

1 In a medium bowl, whisk together eggs, Italian seasoning, cheese, salt, and pepper. Set aside.

2 Press the Sauté button on the Instant Pot® and heat oil. Add bacon and onion and stir-fry 3–4 minutes until onions are translucent and bacon is almost crisp. Press the Cancel button.

3 Transfer cooked mixture to a greased 7-cup glass bowl and set aside to cool 5 minutes. Pour whisked egg mixture over the cooked mixture and stir to combine.

4 Add water to the Instant Pot® and insert steam rack. Place glass bowl with egg mixture on steam rack. Lock lid.

5 Press the Manual or Pressure Cook button and adjust time to 8 minutes. When timer beeps, let pressure release naturally until float valve drops. Unlock lid.

6 Remove bowl from pot and let sit 10 minutes to allow eggs to set. Slice and serve warm.

PER SERVING:

CALORIES: 255 | **FAT:** 18g | **PROTEIN:** 17g | **SODIUM:** 681mg | **FIBER:** 0g | **CARBOHYDRATES:** 3g | **NET CARBS:** 3g | **SUGAR:** 1g

Maple French Toast Casserole

This sweet and delicious breakfast casserole is a treat for any day of the week! Made with simple, easy-to-find ingredients and ready in under a half hour, this dish can be enjoyed any time the urge hits you. You can kick up this breakfast dessert a notch with some fresh whipped cream or a big scoop of vanilla ice cream when no one is looking!

Pantry Staples: granulated sugar, vanilla extract, salt
Hands-On Time: 15 minutes
Cook Time: 20 minutes

Serves 4

4 cups cubed French bread
1 cup whole milk
3 large eggs
1 tablespoon granulated sugar
1 teaspoon vanilla extract
¼ cup pure maple syrup
⅛ teaspoon salt
3 tablespoons unsalted butter, cut into 3 pats
1 cup water

1 Grease a 7-cup glass baking dish. Add bread. Set aside.

2 In a medium bowl, whisk together milk, eggs, sugar, vanilla, maple syrup, and salt. Pour over bread; place butter pats on top.

3 Add water to the Instant Pot® and insert steam rack. Place glass baking dish on top of steam rack. Lock lid.

4 Press the Manual or Pressure Cook button and adjust time to 20 minutes. When timer beeps, quick-release pressure until float valve drops. Unlock lid.

5 Remove bowl and transfer to a cooling rack until set, about 20 minutes. Serve.

PER SERVING:

CALORIES: 356 | FAT: 14g | PROTEIN: 12g | SODIUM: 428mg | FIBER: 1g | CARBOHYDRATES: 43g | NET CARBS: 42g | SUGAR: 20g

Georgia Peach French Toast Casserole

Make sure the peaches you choose for this dish are ripe so you get that natural sweetness. If they aren't quite soft enough and you are ready to make this dessert, add an extra tablespoon or two of sugar to balance out the flavor.

Pantry Staples: vanilla extract, granulated sugar, salt
Hands-On Time: 15 minutes
Cook Time: 20 minutes

Serves 4

4 cups cubed French bread, dried out overnight
2 cups diced, peeled ripe peaches
1 cup whole milk
3 large eggs
1 teaspoon vanilla extract
¼ cup granulated sugar
⅛ teaspoon salt
3 tablespoons unsalted butter, cut into 3 pats
1 cup water

FRENCH BREAD SUBSTITUTIONS

If you don't have a baguette, don't fret. This recipe is excellent with challah, brioche, ciabatta, and even sourdough. And if the bread isn't dried out enough, lightly toast your bread cubes in the oven before assembling the casserole.

1 Grease a 7-cup glass baking dish. Add bread to dish in an even layer. Add peaches in an even layer over bread. Set aside.

2 In a medium bowl, whisk together milk, eggs, vanilla, sugar, and salt. Pour over bread; place butter pats on top.

3 Add water to the Instant Pot® and insert steam rack. Place glass baking dish on top of steam rack. Lock lid.

4 Press the Manual or Pressure Cook button and adjust time to 20 minutes. When timer beeps, quick-release pressure until float valve drops. Unlock lid.

5 Remove bowl and transfer to a cooling rack until set, about 20 minutes. Serve.

PER SERVING:

CALORIES: 371 | FAT: 14g | PROTEIN: 12g | SODIUM: 425mg | FIBER: 2g | CARBOHYDRATES: 47g | NET CARBS: 45g | SUGAR: 24g

Banana Nut Muffins

Banana and walnuts are a classic combination that brings back memories of Grandma-made banana nut breads warm from the oven. Now you can re-create the goodness of those flavors in muffin form in under 10 minutes! Another Instant Pot® miracle!

Pantry Staples: all-purpose baking flour, baking powder, baking soda, salt, vanilla extract, granulated sugar

Hands-On Time: 10 minutes
Cook Time: 9 minutes

Serves 6

1¼ cups all-purpose baking flour
2 teaspoons baking powder
½ teaspoon baking soda
⅛ teaspoon salt
½ teaspoon vanilla extract
3 tablespoons unsalted butter, melted
2 large eggs
¼ cup granulated sugar
2 medium ripe bananas, peeled and mashed with a fork
¼ cup chopped walnuts
1 cup water

1 Grease six silicone cupcake liners.

2 In a large bowl, combine flour, baking powder, baking soda, and salt.

3 In a medium bowl, combine vanilla, butter, eggs, sugar, and bananas.

4 Pour wet ingredients from medium bowl into large bowl with dry ingredients. Gently combine ingredients. Do not overmix. Fold in walnuts, then spoon mixture into prepared cupcake liners.

5 Add water to the Instant Pot® and insert steam rack. Place cupcake liners on top. Lock lid.

6 Press the Manual or Pressure Cook button and adjust time to 9 minutes. When timer beeps, quick-release pressure until float valve drops. Unlock lid.

7 Remove muffins from pot and set aside to cool 30 minutes. Serve.

PER SERVING:

CALORIES: 270 | FAT: 10g | PROTEIN: 6g | SODIUM: 340mg | FIBER: 2g | CARBOHYDRATES: 38g | NET CARBS: 36g | SUGAR: 13g

Cinnamon Roll Doughnut Holes

Who doesn't like doughnut holes for breakfast? Be the hero and whip these up in no time at all in your Instant Pot®! The mix has a lasting shelf life, so this is something you can always have on hand for those times you are in a pinch for something to make for breakfast.

Pantry Staples: none
Hands-On Time: 10 minutes
Cook Time: 16 minutes

Yields 14 doughnut holes

1 (18-ounce) package Krusteaz Cinnamon Roll Supreme Mix (includes icing packet)
6 tablespoons unsalted butter, melted
½ cup cold water
¼ cup chopped pecans
1 cup water

DOUGHNUT OR DONUT?

According to Grammarist .com, "The dictionary-approved spelling for the ring-shaped cake made of dough and fried in fat is *doughnut*. The shortened *donut* has been around since the late 1800s, but it wasn't popularized until the late twentieth century, when the successful American doughnut chain Dunkin' Donuts made it ubiquitous. Today, writers outside the US still favor *doughnut* by a wide margin. *Donut* appears about a third of the time in published American writing."

1 In a medium bowl, combine dry mix, butter, and ½ cup cold water. Fold in pecans. Spoon half of batter into a greased seven-hole silicone egg mold. If your egg mold has a silicone top, use this. If your egg mold came with a plastic top, do not use. Instead, cover with aluminum foil.

2 Add 1 cup water to the Instant Pot® and insert steam rack. Place egg mold on steam rack. Lock lid.

3 Press the Manual or Pressure Cook button and adjust time to 8 minutes. When timer beeps, quick-release pressure until float valve drops. Unlock lid.

4 Pop doughnut holes out of egg mold and repeat with remaining batter.

5 When doughnut holes are cooled, mix icing packet with 1½ tablespoons water and dip doughnut holes into glaze to cover. Serve.

PER SERVING:

CALORIES: 211 | FAT: 9g | PROTEIN: 2g | SODIUM: 300mg | FIBER: 0g | CARBOHYDRATES: 29g | NET CARBS: 29g | SUGAR: 16g

Blueberry-Oat Muffins

Sometimes a healthy on-the-go muffin is the way to go, but often they are full of hard-to-find or expensive ingredients. Luckily, this easy-to-make recipe gives you the antioxidant power of blueberries plus fiber-rich oats to help you feel energized and ready to take on your day—and all with minimal ingredients that you probably already have in your home!

Pantry Staples: all-purpose baking flour, baking powder, baking soda, salt, vanilla extract, granulated sugar
Hands-On Time: 10 minutes
Cook Time: 9 minutes

Serves 6

- 1 cup all-purpose baking flour
- ¼ cup old-fashioned oats
- 2 teaspoons baking powder
- ½ teaspoon baking soda
- ⅛ teaspoon salt
- ½ teaspoon vanilla extract
- 3 tablespoons unsalted butter, melted
- 2 large eggs
- 4 tablespoons granulated sugar
- ⅓ cup blueberries
- 1 cup water

1 Grease six silicone cupcake liners.

2 In a large bowl, combine flour, oats, baking powder, baking soda, and salt.

3 In a medium bowl, combine vanilla, butter, eggs, and sugar.

4 Pour wet ingredients from medium bowl into the bowl with dry ingredients. Gently combine ingredients. Do not overmix. Fold in blueberries, then spoon mixture into prepared cupcake liners.

5 Add water to the Instant Pot® and insert steam rack. Place cupcake liners on top. Lock lid.

6 Press the Manual or Pressure Cook button and adjust time to 9 minutes. When timer beeps, quick-release pressure until float valve drops. Unlock lid.

7 Remove muffins from pot and set aside to cool 30 minutes. Serve.

PER SERVING:

CALORIES: 201 | FAT: 7g | PROTEIN: 5g | SODIUM: 340mg | FIBER: 1g | CARBOHYDRATES: 28g | NET CARBS: 27g | SUGAR: 9g

Pumpkin Muffins

There is a reason that once a year we all go crazy over pumpkin pie spice. It's delicious, and the purée can be added to so many things, which adds another layer of creaminess and nutrition. Put a dollop on your oatmeal, add some to your smoothie, or use it in baking like with these deliciously moist Pumpkin Muffins!

Pantry Staples: all-purpose flour, baking powder, baking soda, salt, vanilla extract
Hands-On Time: 10 minutes
Cook Time: 9 minutes

Serves 6

1¼ cups all-purpose flour
2 teaspoons baking powder
½ teaspoon baking soda
1 teaspoon pumpkin pie spice
⅛ teaspoon salt
¼ cup pumpkin purée
½ teaspoon vanilla extract
1 tablespoon unsalted butter, melted
2 large eggs
⅓ cup packed light brown sugar
1 cup water

ADD IT IN!

If you are looking for a little crunch, fold in ¼ cup chopped nuts to the batter before spooning into cupcake liners. Pecans, walnuts, and almonds all work very well with pumpkin.

1 Grease six silicone cupcake liners.

2 In a large bowl, combine flour, baking powder, baking soda, pumpkin pie spice, and salt.

3 In a medium bowl, combine pumpkin purée, vanilla, butter, eggs, and brown sugar.

4 Pour wet ingredients from medium bowl into large bowl with dry ingredients. Gently combine ingredients. Do not overmix. Spoon mixture into prepared cupcake liners.

5 Add water to the Instant Pot® and insert steam rack. Place cupcake liners on top. Lock lid.

6 Press the Manual or Pressure Cook button and adjust time to 9 minutes. When timer beeps, quick-release pressure until float valve drops. Unlock lid.

7 Remove muffins from pot and set aside to cool 30 minutes. Serve.

PER SERVING:

CALORIES: 188 | FAT: 3g | PROTEIN: 5g | SODIUM: 343mg | FIBER: 1g | CARBOHYDRATES: 33g | NET CARBS: 32g | SUGAR: 12g

3

Soups, Stews, and Chili

Sometimes you may have all of the ingredients for a great soup, but you look at the clock and realize you are only an hour out from dinner. Traditionally, you've needed low heat and a long cooking time to marry together all of the wonderful spices and flavors that make any soup great, but not anymore. The pressurized heat in your Instant Pot® can save the day. Although there is a Slow Cook button on your Instant Pot® for when time isn't an issue, cooking at high pressure can have you serving a finished dinner within an hour. To cut back on time even more, you can find precut onions and peppers in the freezer section of your local grocery store that work great in a pinch.

With Beef Bone Sipping Broth, White Chicken Chili, Homemade Corn Chowder, Senate Bean Soup, and Ramen Noodle Soup, there's something for everyone! So break out your ladle, because dinner is almost ready.

Easy Chicken Broth

Save the carcass of your chicken or two Cornish game hens to make this nutrient- and mineral-packed Easy Chicken Broth that you can use for a soup base in place of store-bought broth.

Pantry Staples: salt
Hands-On Time: 10 minutes
Cook Time: 30 minutes

Serves 4

1 chicken carcass from a
    4-pound whole chicken
2 large carrots, peeled and
    cut into chunks
1 small yellow onion, peeled
    and roughly chopped
2 bay leaves
½ teaspoon apple cider vinegar
1 teaspoon salt
6 cups water

1 Place all ingredients in the Instant Pot®. Lock lid.

2 Press the Manual or Pressure Cook button and adjust time to 30 minutes. When timer beeps, let pressure release naturally until float valve drops. Unlock lid.

3 Use a slotted spoon to retrieve and discard any large items from broth. Strain the remaining liquid through a fine sieve or cheesecloth. Refrigerate broth up to 4 days or freeze up to 6 months.

PER SERVING:

CALORIES: 18 | FAT: 1g | PROTEIN: 2g | SODIUM: 591mg |
FIBER: 0g | CARBOHYDRATES: 1g | NET CARBS: 1g | SUGAR: 0g

Basic Vegetable Broth

There are many reasons to use broth instead of water in dishes. It lends deeper flavors to recipes that use rice, pasta, or mashed tubers, and in stir-fries. Because of this, you may want to change the ingredients in your broth making. For instance, a knob of ginger in your broth may be great for a stir-fry but not in a broccoli soup. So, sub out vegetables and herbs and personalize your broth for different dishes.

Pantry Staples: salt
Hands-On Time: 10 minutes
Cook Time: 30 minutes

Serves 4

- 2 large carrots, peeled and cut into chunks
- 2 medium stalks celery, cut into chunks
- 1 small yellow onion, peeled and chopped
- 1 (1") piece ginger, cleaned and not peeled
- 2 cloves garlic, peeled and halved
- 1 teaspoon salt
- 6 cups water

1 Place all ingredients in the Instant Pot®. Lock lid.

2 Press the Manual or Pressure Cook button and adjust time to 30 minutes. When timer beeps, let pressure release naturally until float valve drops. Unlock lid.

3 Use a slotted spoon to retrieve and discard any large items from broth. Strain the remaining liquid through a fine sieve or cheesecloth. Refrigerate broth up to 4 days or freeze up to 6 months.

PER SERVING:

CALORIES: 5 | FAT: 0g | PROTEIN: 0g | SODIUM: 589mg | FIBER: 0g | CARBOHYDRATES: 1g | NET CARBS: 1g | SUGAR: 1g

FREEZE YOUR BROTH!

How many times have you had leftover broth from a 32-ounce container only for it to go bad? Well, just pour your broth in an ice cube tray or silicone tray. Once the broth is frozen, pop them out and store them in an airtight freezer-safe bag or container. The cubes are great added to sauces, soups, and stir-fries, and even when making rice.

Beef Bone Sipping Broth

Although this is sipping broth, it can still be used in soups, in stews, or however you would traditionally cook with a beef broth. However, enjoy 1–3 cups a day (as you would enjoy warm tea or coffee) for maximum nutritional benefits.

Pantry Staples: salt
Hands-On Time: 10 minutes
Cook Time: 3 hours, 30 minutes

Serves 4

3 pounds grass-fed beef soup bones
2 large carrots, peeled and cut into chunks
1 small yellow onion, peeled and chopped
2 bay leaves
1 tablespoon apple cider vinegar
1 teaspoon salt
6 cups water

1 Preheat oven to 400°F.

2 Place bones on a cookie sheet and bake 30 minutes. Let cool for 10 minutes.

3 Place cooked bones and remaining ingredients in the Instant Pot®. Lock lid.

4 Press the Manual or Pressure Cook button and adjust time to 3 hours. When timer beeps, let pressure release naturally until float valve drops. Unlock lid.

5 Use a slotted spoon to retrieve and discard any large items from broth. Strain the remaining liquid through a fine sieve or cheesecloth. Refrigerate broth up to 4 days or freeze up to 6 months.

PER SERVING:

CALORIES: 50 | FAT: 0g | PROTEIN: 12g | SODIUM: 614mg | FIBER: 0g | CARBOHYDRATES: 1g | NET CARBS: 1g | SUGAR: 0g

WHY DOES BONE BROTH COOK LONGER THAN TRADITIONAL BROTH?

Traditional broth acts as a great base for soups, offers flavoring in stir-fries, and lends depth of flavor to rice dishes. Bone broth, or sipping broth, is cooked longer because the goal is to break down all of the nutrients and gelatin in the bones of the carcass you are cooking. It is slightly higher in calories, but has a significantly higher amount of nutritional benefits.

Potato-Bacon Soup

It is amazing how the modest little potato can be transformed into so many delicious dishes that the world craves. In this case, coupled with some bacon and a few simple spices, your soul will be warmed and happy by this satisfying soup.

Pantry Staples: chicken broth, Italian seasoning, salt, ground black pepper
Hands-On Time: 10 minutes
Cook Time: 20 minutes

Serves 4

2 tablespoons unsalted butter
3 slices bacon, diced
1 small yellow onion, peeled and diced
6 cups diced (½" cubes) Yukon Gold potatoes
4 cups chicken broth
2 teaspoons Italian seasoning
½ teaspoon salt
½ teaspoon ground black pepper
½ cup whole milk

1 Press the Sauté button on the Instant Pot®. Add butter and heat until melted. Add bacon and onion to pot and stir-fry 5 minutes until bacon fat is rendered and onions become translucent.

2 Stir in potatoes, broth, Italian seasoning, salt, and pepper. Press the Cancel button. Lock lid.

3 Press the Manual or Pressure Cook button and adjust time to 15 minutes. When timer beeps, quick-release pressure until float valve drops. Unlock lid.

4 Add milk. Use an immersion blender to blend soup in pot until desired consistency is reached. Or use a stand blender to blend soup in batches.

5 Ladle soup into bowls and serve warm.

PER SERVING:

CALORIES: 352 | FAT: 14g | PROTEIN: 10g | SODIUM: 1,381mg | FIBER: 5g | CARBOHYDRATES: 44g | NET CARBS: 39g | SUGAR: 5g

Tomato Basil Soup

Soup with just a few ingredients? You bet! This is a delicious, creamy, and warming soup that will satisfy even the pickiest of eaters. If you have some crunchy croutons on hand, this is a great place to use them as a garnish. Or you can make a grilled cheese sandwich and cut it into little ½-inch squares for grilled cheese croutons!

Pantry Staples: olive oil, chicken broth, salt, ground black pepper
Hands-On Time: 5 minutes
Cook Time: 13 minutes

Serves 4

1 tablespoon olive oil

1 medium yellow onion, peeled and diced

3 cloves garlic, peeled and minced

2 (15-ounce) cans fire-roasted diced tomatoes, including juice

3 cups chicken broth

¼ cup chopped fresh basil leaves

¾ teaspoon salt

½ teaspoon ground black pepper

½ cup heavy cream

FIRE-ROASTED TOMATOES

Fire-roasted tomatoes can add a smoky charred flavor to your dish. When cooking with a limited amount of ingredients, you'll want to build flavors in your recipes by any means possible. Fire-roasted tomatoes are always a great choice to do this.

1 Press the Sauté button on the Instant Pot® and heat oil. Add onion and stir-fry 3–5 minutes until onions are translucent. Add garlic. Heat an additional 1 minute.

2 Add remaining ingredients, except heavy cream. Press the Cancel button. Lock lid.

3 Press the Manual or Pressure Cook button and adjust time to 7 minutes. When timer beeps, quick-release pressure until float valve drops. Unlock lid.

4 Add heavy cream and purée soup in pot with an immersion blender, or use a stand blender and purée in batches.

5 Ladle into bowls. Serve warm.

PER SERVING:

CALORIES: 210 | FAT: 14g | PROTEIN: 4g | SODIUM: 1,556mg | FIBER: 4g | CARBOHYDRATES: 16g | NET CARBS: 12g | SUGAR: 8g

Lamb Stew

The warmth of this simple stew is excellent served on cold fall nights when you're tucked around a fireplace with friends and family. Or you can whip up a batch of this on St. Paddy's Day and serve it with green beer!

Pantry Staples: all-purpose flour, olive oil, beef broth, Italian seasoning, salt, ground black pepper
Hands-On Time: 15 minutes
Cook Time: 44 minutes

Serves 4

¼ cup all-purpose flour

1 pound cubed boneless lamb

2 tablespoons olive oil

1 medium yellow onion, peeled and diced

2 large carrots, sliced into ½" sections

4 cups beef broth

1 (15-ounce) can fire-roasted diced tomatoes, including juice

2 large Yukon gold potatoes, peeled and cut into ¾" cubes

2 teaspoons Italian seasoning

1 teaspoon salt

½ teaspoon ground black pepper

1 In a medium bowl, toss flour and lamb cubes until lamb is coated.

2 Press the Sauté button on the Instant Pot® and heat oil. Add lamb cubes, searing on all sides for a total of 6 minutes. Set lamb aside. Add onion and carrots and stir-fry 2–3 minutes until onions are translucent.

3 Add broth and deglaze by scraping any bits from the bottom and sides of pot. Stir in remaining ingredients, including lamb. Press the Cancel button. Lock lid.

4 Press the Meat button and cook for the default time of 35 minutes. When timer beeps, let pressure release naturally until float valve drops. Unlock lid.

5 Ladle stew into individual bowls. Serve warm.

PER SERVING:

CALORIES: 437 | FAT: 12g | PROTEIN: 31g | SODIUM: 1,788mg | FIBER: 6g | CARBOHYDRATES: 47g | NET CARBS: 41g | SUGAR: 7g

Old-Fashioned Potato Soup

There is a reason this creamy soup has stood the test of time for decades. It is such an inexpensive soup that requires only a few ingredients. Certainly, you can garnish your bowl with cooked bacon or a dollop of sour cream, but the base soup is just pure comfort food.

Pantry Staples: all-purpose flour, chicken broth, salt, ground black pepper

Hands-On Time: 10 minutes

Cook Time: 10 minutes

Serves 4

- 1 cup whole milk
- 1 tablespoon all-purpose flour
- 6 cups diced (½" cubes) Yukon Gold potatoes
- 3 tablespoons unsalted butter
- 4 cups chicken broth
- 1 teaspoon salt
- 1 teaspoon ground black pepper
- 1 medium yellow onion, peeled and diced
- 1 medium stalk celery, diced

1 In a small bowl, create a slurry by whisking together milk and flour. Set aside in refrigerator.

2 Add remaining ingredients to the Instant Pot®. Lock lid.

3 Press the Manual or Pressure Cook button and adjust time to 10 minutes. When timer beeps, let pressure release naturally for 10 minutes. Quick-release any additional pressure until float valve drops. Unlock lid.

4 Add slurry to pot. Use an immersion blender to blend soup in pot until desired consistency is reached, or use a stand blender to blend soup in batches.

5 Ladle soup into four bowls. Serve warm.

PER SERVING:

CALORIES: 322 | **FAT:** 10g | **PROTEIN:** 9g | **SODIUM:** 1,554mg | **FIBER:** 6g | **CARBOHYDRATES:** 48g | **NET CARBS:** 42g | **SUGAR:** 7g

CELERY STALK GREENS

If your celery has the leaves still attached, don't throw them away. Chop them up and use as a garnish on your soup. Or you can add them to your salad or a homemade pesto, or even set them aside for homemade broths.

Homemade Corn Chowder

After cutting the kernels off of the cobs, you can throw one of the naked cobs in the pot to enhance the flavor. With the remaining cobs, make corn broth. The sweet corn "milk" left in the grooves on the cob creates a delicious golden liquid that can be used instead of water when cooking, or it can be added to another homemade soup.

Pantry Staples: chicken broth, salt, ground black pepper, Italian seasoning
Hands-On Time: 20 minutes
Cook Time: 30 minutes

Serves 4

6 slices bacon

1 large sweet onion, peeled and diced

2 large Yukon Gold potatoes, peeled and diced small

6 cups chicken broth

1 teaspoon salt

1 teaspoon ground black pepper

3 cups (about 5 medium ears corn) fresh corn kernels

1 tablespoon Italian seasoning

1 cup heavy cream

ADD IT IN!

Dice a carrot and/or a celery stalk and add the vegetable(s) when the onion is added to the recipe. Also, use fresh thyme leaves as a tasty garnish.

1   Line a plate with paper towels.

2   Press the Sauté button on the Instant Pot® and fry bacon 2½ minutes. Flip bacon and cook for an additional 2½ minutes. Remove from pot and set on prepared plate.

3   Add onion and sauté 3–5 minutes until onions are translucent. Add potatoes and continue to sauté 2–3 minutes until potatoes start to brown. Add broth, salt, pepper, corn, and Italian seasoning. Crumble 2 bacon pieces and add to pot. Press the Cancel button. Lock lid.

4   Press the Manual or Pressure Cook button and adjust time to 15 minutes. When timer beeps, quick-release pressure until float valve drops. Unlock lid.

5   Add cream and purée soup in pot with an immersion blender, or use a stand blender and purée in batches.

6   Ladle soup into bowls. Crumble remaining bacon slices and distribute on top of each bowl for garnish. Serve warm.

PER SERVING:

CALORIES: 641 | FAT: 38g | PROTEIN: 16g | SODIUM: 2,292mg | FIBER: 6g | CARBOHYDRATES: 58g | NET CARBS: 52g | SUGAR: 13g

White Chicken Chili

You'll want to ladle yourself a bowl of this flavorful, lighter alternative to traditional chili. Top with a dollop of sour cream and maybe a handful of crushed tortilla chips for added crunch. The green chiles added to this dish are very mild, so if you like heat, go ahead and add some red pepper flakes or a little hot sauce.

Pantry Staples: olive oil, chicken broth, salt
Hands-On Time: 15 minutes
Cook Time: 40 minutes

Serves 8

2 teaspoons olive oil
1 pound ground chicken
1 medium yellow onion, peeled and diced
4 cups chicken broth
2 (15-ounce) cans cannellini beans, drained and rinsed
2 (4-ounce) cans diced green chiles, including liquid
1 teaspoon chili powder
1 teaspoon salt

1 Press the Sauté button on the Instant Pot® and heat oil. Add ground chicken and onion and stir-fry approximately 5 minutes until chicken is no longer pink.

2 Stir in remaining ingredients. Press the Cancel button. Lock lid.

3 Press the Meat button and cook for the default time of 35 minutes.

4 When timer beeps, let pressure release naturally until float valve drops. Unlock lid.

5 Ladle chili into individual bowls. Serve warm.

PER SERVING:

CALORIES: 206 | FAT: 6g | PROTEIN: 17g | SODIUM: 1,086mg | FIBER: 6g | CARBOHYDRATES: 20g | NET CARBS: 14g | SUGAR: 4g

Tri-Bean Chili

Game on! Chili is the ultimate crowd-pleaser when the game is on, but who wants to be stuck in the kitchen making it when their favorite team is playing? This chili cooks in the Instant Pot® in half the time of standard chili recipes and uses simple, easy-to-find ingredients as well. Not only is this chili comforting, but your guests can also personalize their dish with simple fixings such as grated cheese, diced red onions, and sour cream.

Pantry Staples: olive oil, hot sauce, garlic salt, beef broth
Hands-On Time: 10 minutes
Cook Time: 30 minutes

Serves 4

- 1 tablespoon olive oil
- 1 small red onion, peeled and diced
- 1 medium green bell pepper, seeded and diced
- 3 (15-ounce) cans tri-bean blend (kidney, pinto, and black beans), drained and rinsed
- 2 tablespoons chili powder
- 1 tablespoon hot sauce
- 1 teaspoon garlic salt
- 1 (28-ounce) can fire-roasted diced tomatoes, including juice
- 3 cups beef broth

1 Press the Sauté button on the Instant Pot® and heat oil. Add onion and bell pepper. Stir-fry 3–5 minutes until onions are translucent.

2 Add remaining ingredients to pot and stir to combine. Press the Cancel button. Lock lid.

3 Press the Manual or Pressure Cook button and adjust time to 25 minutes. When timer beeps, let pressure release naturally until float valve drops. Unlock lid.

4 Ladle chili into bowls. Serve warm.

PER SERVING:

CALORIES: 377 | FAT: 4g | PROTEIN: 23g | SODIUM: 1,979mg | FIBER: 19g | CARBOHYDRATES: 65g | NET CARBS: 46g | SUGAR: 7g

Creamy Chicken Soup

Because chicken thighs are dark meat, they are juicy and full of flavor. On another note, they are also less expensive than chicken breasts. The nourishing nature of this chicken soup is enhanced by adding the bones while cooking, extracting many nutrients for good health.

Pantry Staples: salt, ground black pepper, chicken broth, Italian seasoning
Hands-On Time: 10 minutes
Cook Time: 25 minutes

Serves 4

1 pound bone-in chicken thighs, cut in ½″ cubes (save bones)
1 teaspoon salt
½ teaspoon ground black pepper
2 tablespoons unsalted butter
1 small yellow onion, peeled and diced
1 large carrot, peeled and diced
4 cups chicken broth
1 tablespoon Italian seasoning
½ cup heavy cream

1 Season chicken with salt and pepper.

2 Press the Sauté button on the Instant Pot®. Add butter and heat until melted. Add chicken, onion, and carrot. Sauté 3–5 minutes until onions are translucent. Add broth, Italian seasoning, and chicken bones. Press the Cancel button. Lock lid.

3 Press the Soup button and adjust time to 20 minutes. When timer beeps, let pressure release naturally for 10 minutes. Quick-release any additional pressure until float valve drops. Unlock lid. Remove and discard chicken bones.

4 Stir in cream. Ladle soup into bowls. Serve warm.

PER SERVING:

CALORIES: 359 | FAT: 24g | PROTEIN: 25g | SODIUM: 1,597mg | FIBER: 1g | CARBOHYDRATES: 5g | NET CARBS: 4g | SUGAR: 4g

Split Pea Soup with Ham

Serve sour cream or croutons (or both!) atop this filling and comforting soup. If green soup puts you off, try using yellow split peas. They are actually a little sweeter and milder than the green ones. Follow the recipe in the same manner if using the substitution.

Pantry Staples: olive oil, chicken broth, Italian seasoning, salt, ground black pepper
Hands-On Time: 10 minutes
Cook Time: 35 minutes

Serves 4

1 tablespoon olive oil
1 large sweet onion, peeled and diced
2 medium stalks celery, diced
2 large carrots, peeled and diced
1½ cups dried green split peas, rinsed
5 cups chicken broth
1 teaspoon Italian seasoning
1 pound smoked ham hock
½ teaspoon salt
½ teaspoon ground black pepper

ADD IT IN!
For a fresh take on this rich soup, switch the Italian seasoning with fresh thyme. An easy way to cook with thyme is to tie about four to five thyme sprigs with cooking twine. Add to soup. During the cooking process, the leaves will fall off of the stems, and retrieval of the twined stems is a simple process.

1 Press the Sauté button on the Instant Pot® and heat oil. Add onion, celery, and carrots. Sauté 3–5 minutes until onions are translucent. Add split peas, broth, Italian seasoning, ham hock, salt, and pepper. Press the Cancel button. Lock lid.

2 Press the Soup button and let cook for the default time of 30 minutes. When timer beeps, release pressure naturally for 5 minutes. Quick-release any additional pressure until float valve drops. Unlock lid. Pull ham off of the bone and chop ham into soup.

3 Ladle soup into four bowls. Serve warm.

PER SERVING:

CALORIES: 546 | FAT: 22g | PROTEIN: 33g | SODIUM: 2,604mg | FIBER: 21g | CARBOHYDRATES: 56g | NET CARBS: 35g | SUGAR: 11g

Summer Squash Soup

When your garden is overflowing with yellow squash or zucchini (which can be substituted for squash in this recipe), this quick and easy soup is a tasty solution for your overabundance! With the rich flavors from the bacon and poblano, you won't believe this soup was so simple to make.

Pantry Staples: olive oil, chicken broth, salt, ground black pepper
Hands-On Time: 10 minutes
Cook Time: 24 minutes

Serves 4

1 teaspoon olive oil
3 slices bacon, diced
1 medium sweet onion, peeled and chopped
1 poblano chile pepper, seeded and diced
4 cups diced summer squash
4 cups chicken broth
1 teaspoon salt
½ teaspoon ground black pepper
½ cup heavy cream

1 Line a plate with paper towels.

2 Press the Sauté button on the Instant Pot® and heat oil. Add bacon. Stir-fry 3–4 minutes until just crispy. Set aside on prepared plate.

3 Add onion and poblano chile pepper to pot. Sauté 3–5 minutes until onions are translucent.

4 Add squash, broth, salt, and pepper. Press the Cancel button. Lock lid.

5 Press the Manual or Pressure Cook button and adjust time to 15 minutes. When timer beeps, quick-release pressure until float valve drops. Unlock lid.

6 Add cream. In the Instant Pot®, purée soup with an immersion blender, or use a stand blender and purée in batches until desired consistency is reached.

7 Ladle soup into bowls and garnish with cooked bacon. Serve warm.

PER SERVING:

CALORIES: 208 | FAT: 15g | PROTEIN: 7g | SODIUM: 1,666mg | FIBER: 3g | CARBOHYDRATES: 11g | NET CARBS: 8g | SUGAR: 6g

Senate Bean Soup

If you have a flair for politics, you may enjoy this simple and delicious soup. It has been served every day in the Senate dining room since the early 1900s. The exact source is disputed, but thank goodness the taste of this hearty soup is undisputed!

Pantry Staples: chicken broth, garlic salt, Italian seasoning
Hands-On Time: 5 minutes
Cook Time: 45 minutes

Serves 4

- ½ pound dried great northern beans, rinsed and drained
- 4 cups chicken broth
- 1 cup water
- 1 small yellow onion, peeled and diced
- 3 medium stalks celery, sliced
- ½ teaspoon garlic salt
- 1 smoked ham hock
- 2 tablespoons Italian seasoning

ADD IT IN!

To freshen up this soup, use about ¼ cup chopped fresh parsley instead of the Italian seasoning. Chop a little extra for a pretty garnish!

1 Place all ingredients in the Instant Pot® and stir to combine. Lock lid.

2 Press the Manual or Pressure Cook button and adjust time to 45 minutes. When timer beeps, let pressure release naturally until float valve drops. Unlock lid.

3 Using two forks, shred meat off of ham bone. Discard bone.

4 Ladle soup into bowls. Serve warm.

PER SERVING:

CALORIES: 423 | FAT: 19g | PROTEIN: 27g | SODIUM: 2,307mg | FIBER: 12g | CARBOHYDRATES: 39g | NET CARBS: 27g | SUGAR: 4g

Broccoli-Gruyère Soup

Using Gruyère cheese in this soup that is traditionally made with Cheddar makes you feel like a "grownup" by taking a sophisticated twist! If you need a cheese substitute, try Emmental, Jarlsberg, Beaufort, or even Swiss.

Pantry Staples: chicken broth, salt, ground black pepper
Hands-On Time: 10 minutes
Cook Time: 15 minutes

Serves 4

1 large bunch broccoli, coarsely chopped
1 medium sweet onion, peeled and chopped
4 cups chicken broth
1 teaspoon salt
½ teaspoon ground black pepper
⅛ teaspoon ground nutmeg
½ cup heavy cream
1 cup shredded sharp Gruyère cheese

1 In the Instant Pot®, add broccoli, onion, broth, salt, pepper, and nutmeg. Lock lid.

2 Press the Manual or Pressure Cook button and adjust time to 15 minutes. When timer beeps, quick-release pressure until float valve drops. Unlock lid.

3 Add cream and cheese. In the Instant Pot®, purée the soup with an immersion blender, or use a stand blender and purée in batches until desired consistency is reached.

4 Ladle soup into bowls. Serve warm.

PER SERVING:

CALORIES: 255 | FAT: 19g | PROTEIN: 12g | SODIUM: 1,725mg | FIBER: 2g | CARBOHYDRATES: 8g | NET CARBS: 6g | SUGAR: 4g

Wild Mushroom Soup

Although you can use one type of mushroom in this recipe, using a variety lends a depth of flavor that will make you feel like you're dining in a five-star restaurant.

Pantry Staples: chicken broth, Italian seasoning, salt, ground black pepper
Hands-On Time: 15 minutes
Cook Time: 25 minutes

Serves 4

3 tablespoons unsalted butter
1 small sweet onion, peeled and diced
2 cups sliced mushrooms (shiitake, cremini, portobello, etc.)
4 cups chicken broth
1 tablespoon Italian seasoning
1 teaspoon salt
½ teaspoon ground black pepper
1 cup heavy cream
2 teaspoons cooking sherry

1 Press the Sauté button on the Instant Pot®. Add butter and heat until melted, then add onion. Sauté 3–5 minutes until onions are translucent.

2 Add mushrooms, broth, Italian seasoning, salt, and pepper. Press the Cancel button. Lock lid.

3 Press the Soup button and adjust time to 20 minutes. When timer beeps, let pressure release naturally for 10 minutes. Quick-release any additional pressure until float valve drops. Unlock lid.

4 Add cream and sherry. Use an immersion blender directly in pot to blend soup until desired consistency is reached, either chunky or smooth.

5 Ladle soup into bowls. Serve warm.

PER SERVING:

CALORIES: 312 | FAT: 29g | PROTEIN: 4g | SODIUM: 1,546mg | FIBER: 1g | CARBOHYDRATES: 6g | NET CARBS: 5g | SUGAR: 4g

MUSHROOM VARIETIES
Each variety of mushroom brings a slightly different flavor note. Oyster mushrooms have a bit of a briny note, shiitakes have a smoky hint, and morels have a fabulous nuttiness. Change up the mushrooms that you use in this recipe for a true "wild mushroom" blend for balance and flavor.

Chicken Taco Soup

Flavorful, delicious, and hearty, this soup is a crowd-pleaser, and it uses only minimal ingredients. The variety of flavors and textures will have your family wishing you had made a double batch!

Pantry Staples: olive oil, chicken broth, salt, ground black pepper
Hands-On Time: 15 minutes
Cook Time: 25 minutes

Serves 4

1 tablespoon olive oil
1 small red onion, peeled and diced
1 (28-ounce) can diced tomatoes, including juice
3 cups chicken broth
½ pound boneless, skinless chicken breasts
2 tablespoons taco seasoning
½ teaspoon salt
¼ teaspoon ground black pepper
½ cup chopped fresh cilantro, divided

1   Press the Sauté button on the Instant Pot® and heat oil. Add onion. Sauté 3–5 minutes until onions are translucent.

2   Add tomatoes and broth; deglaze pot by scraping up any bits from the bottom and sides of pot.

3   Add chicken, taco seasoning, salt, pepper, and ¼ cup cilantro. Press the Cancel button. Lock lid.

4   Press the Manual or Pressure Cook button and adjust time to 15 minutes. When timer beeps, quick-release pressure until float valve drops. Unlock lid. Use two forks to shred chicken in pot. Let simmer 5 minutes.

5   Ladle soup into bowls and garnish with remaining cilantro. Serve warm.

PER SERVING:

CALORIES: 196 | **FAT:** 5g | **PROTEIN:** 21g | **SODIUM:** 1,682mg | **FIBER:** 4g | **CARBOHYDRATES:** 15g | **NET CARBS:** 11g | **SUGAR:** 7g

ADD IT IN!

This soup can be taken to the next level by adding a can of drained corn, black or green olives, and a diced jalapeño during the cooking process. Also, offer garnishes such as diced avocados, crumbled tortilla chips, or sour cream!

Ramen Noodle Soup

Ramen Eggs (see recipe in Chapter 6) would be a tasty substitute for the Hard-"Boiled" Eggs called for in this recipe. You can find ramen broth in the soup aisle of most mainstream grocery stores. There are also many recipes online, so if you'd like to make your own from scratch, you can!

Pantry Staples: olive oil
Hands-On Time: 10 minutes
Cook Time: 10 minutes

Serves 4

- 2 teaspoons olive oil
- 4 medium green onions, sliced (whites and greens separated)
- 4 ounces shiitake mushrooms, sliced
- 4 cups ramen broth
- 1 (10.75-ounce) package ramen noodles
- 2 Hard-"Boiled" Eggs (see recipe in Chapter 2), peeled and halved

ADD IT IN!

If you have sesame oil on hand, substitute it for the olive oil. For more depth of flavor, add a tablespoon of soy sauce to the broth before cooking. For a kick, add a tablespoon or two of sriracha or gochujang and adjust the heat to your personal liking.

1 Press the Sauté button on the Instant Pot® and heat oil. Add onion whites and mushrooms. Sauté 3–5 minutes until onions are translucent. Add broth and noodles. Press the Cancel button. Lock lid.

2 Press the Manual or Pressure Cook button and adjust time to 5 minutes. When timer beeps, quick-release pressure until float valve drops. Unlock lid.

3 Ladle soup into bowls. Garnish each bowl with an egg half and onion greens. Serve warm.

PER SERVING:

CALORIES: 432 | FAT: 18g | PROTEIN: 13g | SODIUM: 1,978mg | FIBER: 4g | CARBOHYDRATES: 52g | NET CARBS: 48g | SUGAR: 4g

Cajun Andouille Sausage Gumbo

Enjoy this Cajun cuisine as is or served over a scoop of white rice. The roux, created from oil and flour, mixes with the Louisiana trinity (onion, celery, and bell pepper) to give this dish the soup base that will have you hollering, "Ca c'est bon!"

Pantry Staples: olive oil, all-purpose flour, chicken broth, Italian seasoning
Hands-On Time: 15 minutes
Cook Time: 23 minutes

Serves 4

- ¼ cup olive oil
- ¼ cup all-purpose flour
- 1 medium yellow onion, peeled and diced
- 2 medium stalks celery, diced
- 1 small green bell pepper, seeded and diced
- 4 cups chicken broth
- 1 pound smoked andouille sausage, sliced
- 1 tablespoon gumbo filé
- 1 tablespoon Italian seasoning

WHAT IS GUMBO FILÉ?

Also known as *filé powder*, this herbal powder is made from the dried and ground leaves of the sassafras tree. It not only adds flavor to many dishes native to Louisiana, but it also acts as a thickener.

1 Press the Sauté button on the Instant Pot®. Add oil and flour and whisk them together while cooking, about 4 minutes; the mixture will deepen in color. Add onion, celery, and bell pepper; sauté an additional 4 minutes.

2 Whisk in broth and deglaze pot by scraping up brown bits from the bottom and sides of pot. Add remaining ingredients. Press the Cancel button. Lock lid.

3 Press the Soup button and adjust time to 15 minutes. When timer beeps, let pressure release naturally for 5 minutes. Quick-release any additional pressure until float valve drops. Unlock lid.

4 Ladle gumbo into bowls. Serve warm.

PER SERVING:

CALORIES: 406 | FAT: 31g | PROTEIN: 21g | SODIUM: 2,251mg | FIBER: 4g | CARBOHYDRATES: 14g | NET CARBS: 10g | SUGAR: 3g

4

Beans, Rice, and Grains

Want to save some money? Hello, Instant Pot®! Those 90-second microwavable rice packets are certainly easy, but they are highly processed and the price tag reflects it. Want to buy those beans in bulk but know that you'll never get around to soaking them? Fortunately, your Instant Pot® can solve these problems, and you'll not only be eating beans and rice for pennies on the dollar, but the prep and cooking time is lowered drastically as well.

And don't forget about the pasta that can be cooked to perfection in the Instant Pot®. The pressure and steam create deliciously moist and tender side dishes and meals. From Salsa Rice to Seasoned Black-Eyed Peas, and from Confetti Quinoa to Cheeseburger Macaroni, you'll be whipping up some new and tasty dishes with ease.

Basic Basmati White Rice

Traditionally served with Indian and South Asian recipes, long-grained basmati rice is really making its way into everyday American cooking. It is a fluffy and aromatic swap for short-grain white rice.

Pantry Staples: chicken broth, salt
Hands-On Time: 2 minutes
Cook Time: 5 minutes

Serves 4

2 cups basmati rice
1¼ cups water
1 cup chicken broth
1 teaspoon salt
1 tablespoon unsalted butter

1 Optional step: Some people like to soak their rice in water 1 hour to reduce impurities. If you do this, decrease water added to pot from 1¼ cups to 1 cup.

2 Place all ingredients in the Instant Pot®. Lock lid.

3 Press the Manual or Pressure Cook button and adjust time to 5 minutes. When timer beeps, let pressure release naturally until float valve drops. Unlock lid.

4 Serve warm.

PER SERVING:

CALORIES: 348 | FAT: 3g | PROTEIN: 8g | SODIUM: 812mg | FIBER: 2g | CARBOHYDRATES: 70g | NET CARBS: 68g | SUGAR: 0g

Basic Risotto

Although this is a basic risotto recipe, there is nothing basic about risotto. Creamy and starchy, this is a great base for many add-ins from vegetables to lobster meat.

Pantry Staples: chicken broth, salt, ground black pepper
Hands-On Time: 5 minutes
Cook Time: 19 minutes

Serves 4

- 4 tablespoons unsalted butter
- 1 small yellow onion, peeled and finely diced
- 2 cloves garlic, peeled and minced
- 1½ cups Arborio rice
- 4 cups chicken broth, divided
- 3 tablespoons grated Parmesan cheese
- ½ teaspoon salt
- ¼ teaspoon ground black pepper

1 Press the Sauté button on the Instant Pot®. Add butter and heat until melted. Add onion and stir-fry 3–5 minutes until onions are translucent. Add garlic and rice and cook an additional 1 minute.

2 Add 1 cup broth and stir 2–3 minutes until it is absorbed by rice.

3 Add remaining 3 cups broth, cheese, salt, and pepper. Press the Cancel button. Lock lid.

4 Press the Manual or Pressure Cook button and adjust time to 10 minutes. When timer beeps, let pressure release naturally for 10 minutes. Quick-release any additional pressure until float valve drops. Unlock lid.

5 Ladle risotto into bowls. Serve warm.

PER SERVING:

CALORIES: 414 | **FAT:** 12g | **PROTEIN:** 8g | **SODIUM:** 1,285mg | **FIBER:** 3g | **CARBOHYDRATES:** 64g | **NET CARBS:** 61g | **SUGAR:** 2g

Weeknight Baked Beans

These beans make a perfect busy weeknight side dish that is great with burgers or hot dogs. This recipe uses canned beans and bottled barbecue sauce to cut down on your kitchen time, which allows you to spend more time on what means the most to you.

Pantry Staples: olive oil, salt, ground black pepper
Hands-On Time: 10 minutes
Cook Time: 8 minutes

Serves 6

2 teaspoons olive oil
2 slices bacon, diced
1 (15-ounce) can great northern beans, drained and rinsed
1 (15-ounce) can pinto beans, drained and rinsed
1 teaspoon salt
¼ teaspoon ground black pepper
½ cup molasses barbecue sauce
1 tablespoon yellow mustard
1 cup water

1   Line a plate with paper towels.

2   Press the Sauté button on the Instant Pot® and heat oil. Add bacon. Stir-fry 3–5 minutes until bacon is almost crisp. Transfer bacon to prepared plate to absorb grease. Press the Cancel button. Rinse pot.

3   In a 7-cup glass baking dish, add bacon, beans, salt, pepper, barbecue sauce, and mustard.

4   Add water to the Instant Pot® and insert steam rack. Place glass baking dish on top of steam rack. Lock lid.

5   Press the Manual or Pressure Cook button and adjust time to 3 minutes. When timer beeps, quick-release pressure until float valve drops. Unlock lid.

6   Transfer beans to a bowl. Serve warm.

PER SERVING:

CALORIES: 224 | **FAT:** 3g | **PROTEIN:** 11g | **SODIUM:** 567mg | **FIBER:** 5g | **CARBOHYDRATES:** 38g | **NET CARBS:** 33g | **SUGAR:** 10g

Basic Couscous

Couscous is small granules of pasta made from semolina flour. Serve this recipe as a side dish or add some meat and vegetables during the cooking process for a complete meal.

Pantry Staples: chicken broth, salt
Hands-On Time: 5 minutes
Cook Time: 4 minutes

Serves 6

2 cups couscous
2½ cups water
1 cup chicken broth
1 teaspoon salt
1 tablespoon unsalted butter
1 teaspoon lemon zest

1   Place all ingredients in the Instant Pot®. Lock lid.

2   Press the Manual or Pressure Cook button and adjust time to 4 minutes. When timer beeps, let pressure release naturally until float valve drops. Unlock lid.

3   Serve warm.

PER SERVING:

CALORIES: 235 | FAT: 2g | PROTEIN: 8g | SODIUM: 547mg | FIBER: 3g | CARBOHYDRATES: 45g | NET CARBS: 42g | SUGAR: 0g

Salsa Rice

It doesn't get any easier than this. This is a great side for Taco Tuesday or to accompany a juicy steak. There's no chopping or prep work. Just add ingredients to the Instant Pot® and let it do its work!

Pantry Staples: chicken broth, salt, ground black pepper
Hands-On Time: 10 minutes
Cook Time: 15 minutes

Serves 6

1 cup basmati rice
1 cup chicken broth
1 (15.5-ounce) jar chunky salsa
1 teaspoon salt
½ teaspoon ground black pepper

1 Place all ingredients in the Instant Pot®. Lock lid.

2 Press the Rice button. (The Instant Pot® will determine the cooking time, about 15 minutes.) When timer beeps, let pressure release naturally for 10 minutes. Quick-release any additional pressure until float valve drops. Unlock lid.

3 Transfer rice to a dish. Serve warm.

PER SERVING:

CALORIES: 127 | FAT: 0g | PROTEIN: 3g | SODIUM: 1,067mg | FIBER: 3g | CARBOHYDRATES: 28g | NET CARBS: 25g | SUGAR: 5g

Spiced Green Lentils

Although lentils make an excellent side dish, these small seeds categorized as legumes are high in protein and fiber. Because of this, they are worthy enough to be served alone on Meatless Mondays!

Pantry Staples: chicken broth, salt, ground black pepper
Hands-On Time: 5 minutes
Cook Time: 9 minutes

Serves 4

1 cup dried green lentils
1½ cups chicken broth
½ cup tomato sauce
1 tablespoon lemon juice
1 teaspoon ground cumin
½ teaspoon garlic powder
¼ teaspoon salt
¼ teaspoon ground black
   pepper

1 Add lentils and broth to the Instant Pot®. Lock lid.

2 Press the Manual or Pressure Cook button and adjust time to 9 minutes. When timer beeps, quick-release pressure until float valve drops. Unlock lid. Stir in additional ingredients.

3 Transfer lentils to a dish. Serve warm.

PER SERVING:

CALORIES: 186 | FAT: 1g | PROTEIN: 13g | SODIUM: 640mg | FIBER: 6g | CARBOHYDRATES: 33g | NET CARBS: 27g | SUGAR: 3g

Red Beans and Chorizo

Only have a few ingredients but still want to take a virtual taste trip to New Orleans? These red beans will fulfill your craving. Serve this dish with a scoop of rice for the full experience!

Pantry Staples: olive oil, chicken broth, salt
Hands-On Time: 15 minutes
Cook Time: 35 minutes

Serves 8

- 1 tablespoon olive oil
- 1 small yellow onion, peeled and diced
- ½ pound chorizo, loose or removed from casing
- 1 cup dried red beans, rinsed and drained
- 3 cups chicken broth
- 1 (14.5-ounce) can diced tomatoes, including juice
- ½ teaspoon salt
- 1 tablespoon Creole seasoning

1 Press the Sauté button on the Instant Pot® and heat oil. Add onion and chorizo. Stir-fry 3–5 minutes until onions are translucent. Add broth and deglaze by scraping the bottom and sides of pot.

2 Add beans and remaining ingredients. Press the Cancel button. Lock lid.

3 Press the Bean button and cook for the default time of 30 minutes. When timer beeps, let pressure release naturally for 10 minutes. Quick-release any additional pressure until float valve drops. Unlock lid.

4 Using a slotted spoon, transfer beans to a serving bowl. Let cool to thicken, about 10 minutes, then serve.

PER SERVING:

CALORIES: 242 | FAT: 12g | PROTEIN: 13g | SODIUM: 1,463mg | FIBER: 4g | CARBOHYDRATES: 18g | NET CARBS: 14g | SUGAR: 3g

ADD IT IN!

If you want to bump up this hearty dish of beans, add two diced celery stalks to the step in the recipe where you add the onion. Also, stir in a handful of chopped parsley or cilantro after you unlock the lid.

Minty Feta and Tomato Couscous Salad

This Greek flavor–inspired chilled salad is so incredibly fresh tasting! Make this for your friends on a hot day while dining on the deck. It's not too heavy, not too light. And it's so easy, you can prepare it the night before!

Pantry Staples: olive oil, salt
Hands-On Time: 15 minutes
Cook Time: 9 minutes

Serves 6

3 tablespoons olive oil, divided
1 cup pearl couscous
2 cups water
2 small Roma tomatoes, seeded and diced
¼ cup chopped fresh mint leaves
Juice and zest of 1 small lemon
¼ cup feta cheese
½ teaspoon salt

ADD IT IN!

For an extra layer of crunch and flavor, dice an English cucumber into this salad. The English cucumber has fewer and smaller seeds than a regular cucumber, which makes it easier to eat. You can find these in the produce section, wrapped in plastic to protect their delicate thin skin. Diced Kalamata olives would also be a welcomed addition to this dish.

1. Press the Sauté button on the Instant Pot® and heat 1 tablespoon oil. Add couscous and stir-fry 2–4 minutes until couscous is slightly browned. Add water. Press the Cancel button. Lock lid.

2. Press the Manual or Pressure Cook button and adjust time to 5 minutes. When timer beeps, let pressure release naturally for 5 minutes. Quick-release any additional pressure until float valve drops. Unlock lid. Drain any liquid.

3. In a medium bowl, combine remaining ingredients, including remaining olive oil. Set aside. Once couscous has cooled, toss it into bowl with other ingredients. Cover and refrigerate overnight until ready to be served chilled.

PER SERVING:

CALORIES: 189 | FAT: 8g | PROTEIN: 5g | SODIUM: 254mg | FIBER: 2g | CARBOHYDRATES: 24g | NET CARBS: 22g | SUGAR: 1g

Dried Cherry and Pistachio Quinoa Salad

So many flavors and textures, so few ingredients! You get tartness and a little chewiness from the cherries, acid from the lime, smokiness from the cumin, and crunch from the pistachios. Mixed together with the fiber-rich quinoa, this salad is an absolute powerhouse!

Pantry Staples: olive oil, salt
Hands-On Time: 5 minutes
Cook Time: 20 minutes

Serves 4

1 cup quinoa
1¾ cups water
Juice and zest from 1 medium lime, separated
2 tablespoons olive oil
¼ cup chopped dried cherries
¼ cup chopped pistachios
1 teaspoon ground cumin
½ teaspoon salt

1   Add quinoa, water, and lime juice to the Instant Pot®. Stir well. Lock lid.

2   Press the Porridge button and cook for the default time of 20 minutes. When timer beeps, quick-release pressure until float valve drops. Unlock lid.

3   Transfer quinoa to a serving dish and fluff with a fork. Toss in lime zest and remaining ingredients. Serve chilled.

PER SERVING:

CALORIES: 295 | FAT: 12g | PROTEIN: 8g | SODIUM: 295mg | FIBER: 4g | CARBOHYDRATES: 38g | NET CARBS: 34g | SUGAR: 7g

Butter Beans and Hog Jowl

Butter beans are actually lima beans, just larger and with an off-white color. Their texture is creamy, and they have an almost buttery flavor—hence the name! With the addition of the salty hog jowl, this will soon be your new favorite bean side dish.

Pantry Staples: ground black pepper, chicken broth
Hands-On Time: 10 minutes
Cook Time: 35 minutes

Serves 6

2½ cups (16-ounce bag) dried large butter beans, rinsed, drained, and picked over for undesirables
1 medium sweet onion, peeled and diced
1 (4-ounce) smoked hog jowl, diced
½ teaspoon ground black pepper
2 cups water
2 cups chicken broth

WHAT IS A HOG JOWL?
Also known as *pork jowl* or *jowl bacon*, it is essentially the meat from a pig's cheek that has been cured and smoked. It lends a great smoky and salty flavor to beans and soups.

1 Place all ingredients in the Instant Pot®. Lock lid.

2 Press the Manual or Pressure Cook button and adjust time to 35 minutes. When timer beeps, let pressure release naturally for 10 minutes. Quick-release any additional pressure until float valve drops. Unlock lid. Drain any excess liquid.

3 Transfer beans to a large bowl. Serve warm.

PER SERVING:

CALORIES: 382 | FAT: 13g | PROTEIN: 18g | SODIUM: 542mg | FIBER: 14g | CARBOHYDRATES: 49g | NET CARBS: 35g | SUGAR: 7g

Seasoned Black-Eyed Peas

There ain't nothing better than a side of black-eyed peas, especially if it is next to some collard greens and a hush puppy. This recipe doesn't call for salt, because ham hocks can be a little salty. Before serving, take a quick taste and add a pinch or two of salt if needed.

Pantry Staples: olive oil, ground black pepper, chicken broth
Hands-On Time: 10 minutes
Cook Time: 36 minutes

Serves 8

- 1 tablespoon olive oil
- 1 large sweet onion, peeled and diced
- 1 medium stalk celery, diced
- 4 cloves garlic, peeled and minced
- 2 cups dried black-eyed peas
- 1 ham hock
- ¼ teaspoon ground black pepper
- 4 cups chicken broth

1 Press the Sauté button on the Instant Pot® and heat oil. Add onion and celery. Stir-fry 3–5 minutes until onions are translucent. Add garlic and heat an additional 1 minute. Add black-eyed peas, ham hock, pepper, and broth. Toss to combine. Press the Cancel button. Lock lid.

2 Press the Manual or Pressure Cook button and adjust time to 30 minutes. When timer beeps, let pressure release naturally for 5 minutes. Quick-release any additional pressure until float valve drops. Unlock lid.

3 Dice meat off of ham hock and discard bone. Return ham to pot and stir. Using a slotted spoon, transfer ingredients from pot to a large bowl. Serve warm.

PER SERVING:

CALORIES: 167 | FAT: 11g | PROTEIN: 8g | SODIUM: 1,021mg | FIBER: 2g | CARBOHYDRATES: 10g | NET CARBS: 8g | SUGAR: 3g

Confetti Quinoa

You can absolutely just use one color of bell pepper for this dish if that's what you have on hand. But if you are going for a little flair, add a little of each color for fun! Also, there really is a difference in taste. Red peppers are the sweetest, with orange and yellow at a close second. The green bell peppers have a bitter note because they are not as ripe as the others.

Pantry Staples: salt, olive oil
Hands-On Time: 5 minutes
Cook Time: 20 minutes

Serves 4

1 cup quinoa
1¾ cups water
¼ cup lemon juice
½ teaspoon salt
2 tablespoons olive oil
¼ cup small-diced green bell pepper
¼ cup small-diced red bell pepper
¼ cup small-diced yellow bell pepper

1 Add quinoa, water, and lemon juice to the Instant Pot®. Stir well. Lock lid.

2 Press the Porridge button and cook for the default time of 20 minutes. When timer beeps, quick-release pressure until float valve drops. Unlock lid.

3 Transfer quinoa to a serving dish and fluff with a fork. Toss in salt, oil, and bell peppers. Serve warm.

PER SERVING:

CALORIES: 223 | FAT: 9g | PROTEIN: 6g | SODIUM: 293mg | FIBER: 3g | CARBOHYDRATES: 29g | NET CARBS: 26g | SUGAR: 1g

Cheeseburger Macaroni

I mean...cheeseburger...macaroni...yes! After a week of trying to feed your family broccoli and grilled chicken, sometimes you just need a night of no complaining. This dish will fit the bill. If you want to go full cheeseburger, serve a bowl of this with some diced pickles, shredded lettuce, and a drizzle of yellow mustard!

Pantry Staples: olive oil, salt, ground black pepper
Hands-On Time: 5 minutes
Cook Time: 9 minutes

Serves 4

1 tablespoon olive oil
1 pound 80/20 ground beef
1 pound elbow macaroni
¼ cup whole milk
1½ cups shredded sharp Cheddar cheese
2 tablespoons unsalted butter
2 teaspoons salt
½ teaspoon ground black pepper

1 Press the Sauté button on the Instant Pot® and heat oil. Add ground beef. Stir-fry 5 minutes until browned. Press the Cancel button. Using a slotted spoon, transfer beef to a medium bowl. Set aside. Clean grease from pot.

2 Place macaroni in an even layer in pot. Pour enough water to come about ¼" over pasta. Lock lid.

3 Press the Manual or Pressure Cook button and adjust time to 4 minutes. When timer beeps, let pressure release naturally for 3 minutes. Quick-release any additional pressure until float valve drops. Unlock lid.

4 Drain any residual water. Add milk, cheese, butter, salt, and pepper. Add in cooked ground beef. Stir in the warmed pot until well combined. Serve warm.

PER SERVING:

CALORIES: 889 | FAT: 34g | PROTEIN: 46g | SODIUM: 1,518mg | FIBER: 4g | CARBOHYDRATES: 86g | NET CARBS: 84g | SUGAR: 4g

Creamy Polenta

This savory polenta dish is excellent as a side dish or a tasty base for steamed shrimp or grilled sausage (or both).

Pantry Staples: salt, ground black pepper
Hands-On Time: 5 minutes
Cook Time: 15 minutes

Serves 6

3 cups water
1 cup whole milk
1 cup coarse ground yellow polenta
1 teaspoon salt
¼ teaspoon ground black pepper
2 tablespoons unsalted butter
¼ cup grated Parmesan cheese

1 Add water, milk, polenta, salt, and pepper to the Instant Pot® and stir. Lock lid.

2 Press the Manual or Pressure Cook button and adjust time to 10 minutes. When timer beeps, quick-release pressure until float valve drops. Unlock lid.

3 Whisk butter and cheese into polenta in pot up to 5 minutes until it thickens.

4 Transfer polenta to a serving dish. Serve warm.

PER SERVING:

CALORIES: 149 | FAT: 6g | PROTEIN: 4g | SODIUM: 487mg | FIBER: 2g | CARBOHYDRATES: 18g | NET CARBS: 16g | SUGAR: 2g

POLENTA, GRITS, AND CORNMEAL—ARE THEY DIFFERENT?

All three of these products are made from ground corn. Cornmeal is the finest version of the three. Grits are ground down from white corn, otherwise known as *hominy*. Polenta has a little coarser grind than grits and is made from yellow corn. Know these distinctions when purchasing the products, because sometimes polenta is labeled as "coarse ground cornmeal"!

Bow Tie Pasta Marinara

Also known as *farfalle* or *butterfly pasta*, bow tie pasta just puts a smile on your face. One, it's pasta. Two, it's cute. And the ease of this dish topped with fresh ingredients makes this a home run. You'd never guess it uses a bottled tomato sauce!

Pantry Staples: olive oil
Hands-On Time: 10 minutes
Cook Time: 13 minutes

Serves 4

1 tablespoon olive oil
1 small yellow onion, peeled and diced
1 pound bow tie pasta
1 (24-ounce) jar marinara sauce
¼ cup grated Parmesan cheese
¼ cup chiffonade of basil

WHAT IS A CHIFFONADE OF BASIL?

Basically, a chiffonade is a cutting technique slicing delicate leaves into thin ribbons. Position your basil leaves on top of one another. Roll them into a cigar shape. Using a sharp knife, slice into thin ribbons. A sharp knife is key here; otherwise, you will bruise the delicate leaves.

1 Press the Sauté button on the Instant Pot® and heat oil. Add onion and stir-fry 3–5 minutes until onions are translucent.

2 Place pasta over cooked onions in an even layer in pot. Pour enough water to come about ¼" over pasta. Press the Cancel button. Lock lid.

3 Press the Manual or Pressure Cook button and adjust time to 3 minutes. When timer beeps, let pressure release naturally for 3 minutes. Quick-release any additional pressure until float valve drops. Press the Cancel button. Unlock lid. Drain any residual water.

4 Pour sauce over pasta and stir. Press the Sauté button on the Instant Pot®, press the Adjust button to change temperature to Less, and simmer unlidded 5 minutes to warm the sauce. Stir, then transfer to dishes.

5 Garnish with cheese and basil. Serve warm.

PER SERVING:

CALORIES: 567 | FAT: 8g | PROTEIN: 19g | SODIUM: 832mg | FIBER: 7g | CARBOHYDRATES: 100g | NET CARBS: 93g | SUGAR: 13g

Amish-Inspired Egg Noodles

These noodles are Amish-"inspired" because the Amish usually make these egg noodles from scratch with four simple ingredients—flour, salt, eggs, and water. We are skipping that step! But, luckily for you, egg noodles are sold dried in the pasta aisle and are a tasty diversion from traditional pasta.

Pantry Staples: chicken broth, salt, ground black pepper
Hands-On Time: 2 minutes
Cook Time: 4 minutes

Serves 6

1 (12-ounce) bag egg noodles
2 cups chicken broth
4 tablespoons unsalted butter
½ teaspoon salt
¼ teaspoon ground black pepper
¼ cup chopped fresh parsley

1 Place noodles in an even layer in the Instant Pot®. Pour broth over noodles. Add enough water for liquid to come about ¼″ over noodles. Lock lid.

2 Press the Manual or Pressure Cook button and adjust time to 4 minutes. When timer beeps, let pressure release naturally for 3 minutes. Quick-release any additional pressure until float valve drops. Unlock lid.

3 Drain any residual water. Toss noodles with butter, salt, pepper, and parsley. Serve warm.

PER SERVING:

CALORIES: 286 | FAT: 10g | PROTEIN: 9g | SODIUM: 508mg | FIBER: 2g | CARBOHYDRATES: 39g | NET CARBS: 37g | SUGAR: 2g

Cajun Red Beans

Not having to soak beans overnight is a time-saver, especially when you want to eat the beans that same day. Enjoy these Cajun beans as a side dish, as a main dish, over rice, or even as a New Orleans twist with the humble taco.

Pantry Staples: olive oil, vegetable broth, garlic salt, Italian seasoning
Hands-On Time: 5 minutes
Cook Time: 40 minutes

Serves 4

1 tablespoon olive oil
½ small yellow onion, peeled and diced
1 small red bell pepper, seeded and diced
1 medium stalk celery, diced
3 cups vegetable broth
1 cup (about ½ pound) dried red kidney beans, rinsed and drained
1 teaspoon Cajun seasoning
½ teaspoon garlic salt
2 teaspoons Italian seasoning

ADDING VINEGAR TO BEANS
After your beans have finished cooking, add about 1 teaspoon of apple cider vinegar per cup of dried beans to the end cooked product. The vinegar helps with digestion by breaking down some of the natural sugars in the beans. Also, a hit of acid to any dish always helps balance flavors, enhancing the taste of the dish.

1 Press the Sauté button on the Instant Pot® and heat oil. Add onion, bell pepper, and celery. Stir-fry 3–5 minutes until onions are translucent. Deglaze pot by adding broth and scraping the bottom and sides of pot.

2 Add beans, Cajun seasoning, garlic salt, and Italian seasoning. Press the Cancel button. Lock lid.

3 Press the Manual or Pressure Cook button and cook for 35 minutes. When timer beeps, let pressure release naturally for 10 minutes. Quick-release any additional pressure until float valve drops. Unlock lid.

4 With a slotted spoon, transfer beans to a serving dish. Serve warm.

PER SERVING:

CALORIES: 202 | FAT: 4g | PROTEIN: 11g | SODIUM: 919mg | FIBER: 8g | CARBOHYDRATES: 32g | NET CARBS: 24g | SUGAR: 4g

5

Appetizers

Appetizers can be served before the main meal or as bite-sized treats at a gathering or cocktail party. In either case, you are usually making them for a special occasion, which means cleaning the house, spending extra on food, and getting yourself ready on top of that. This chapter introduces some delicious recipes that will save you time in the kitchen as well as money because of the simple number of ingredients.

With crowd-pleasing appetizers such as Mini Corn Dog Bites, Classic Buffalo Chicken Wings, and Warm Shrimp Dip, the only problem you'll have incorporating the recipes in this chapter into your next social event will be deciding which ones to make.

BBQ Cocktail Weenies

People have been crowding around this appetizer for decades! The old recipes were a basic combination of grape jelly and chili sauce—don't you just love the '70s? This version is a bit more sophisticated than that but with just as few ingredients!

Pantry Staples: none
Hands-On Time: 10 minutes
Cook Time: 15 minutes

Serves 8

1½ cups barbecue sauce
1 cup Dr Pepper
1 tablespoon Dijon mustard
1 (24-ounce) package beef little smokies

1 In a medium bowl, whisk together barbecue sauce, Dr Pepper, and mustard.

2 Add smokies to the Instant Pot®. Pour in barbecue sauce mixture. Lock lid.

3 Press the Manual or Pressure Cook button and adjust time to 15 minutes. When timer beeps, quick-release pressure until float valve drops. Unlock lid.

4 Serve warm with toothpicks.

PER SERVING:

CALORIES: 360 | FAT: 22g | PROTEIN: 11g | SODIUM: 1,420mg | FIBER: 0g | CARBOHYDRATES: 27g | NET CARBS: 27g | SUGAR: 22g

Mini Corn Dog Bites

Sometimes cute food is the best food! Little effort brings big results with this recipe. These miniature comfort-food appetizers will bring smiles to many faces—from kids to adults—and are sure to bring praise to the chef!

Pantry Staples: none
Hands-On Time: 10 minutes
Cook Time: 26 minutes

Serves 4

1 (8.5-ounce) box Jiffy Corn Muffin Mix
1 large egg
⅓ cup whole milk
14 mini craft sticks
4 hot dogs, cut in thirds
1 cup water

WHAT ARE MINI CRAFT STICKS?

Mini craft sticks are simply short ice-cream sticks. They can be found in craft stores, online, and in the craft aisle of big-box stores.

1 Grease a seven-hole silicone egg mold.

2 In a medium bowl, combine corn muffin mix, egg, and milk. Fill an egg mold compartment halfway with batter. Press a craft stick into the end of a hot dog section and press into the middle of batter. Repeat with remaining compartments.

3 Add water to the Instant Pot® and insert steam rack. Place filled egg mold on steam rack. Lock lid.

4 Press the Manual or Pressure Cook button and adjust time to 13 minutes. When timer beeps, quick-release pressure until float valve drops. Unlock lid.

5 After 2–3 minutes, pop corn dog bites out of egg mold and transfer to a plate. Repeat with remaining batter.

6 Serve warm.

PER SERVING:

CALORIES: 431 | FAT: 22g | PROTEIN: 10g | SODIUM: 1,026mg | FIBER: 0g | CARBOHYDRATES: 45g | NET CARBS: 45g | SUGAR: 13g

Mini Meatball Sliders

Meat, sauce, and bread! Yep, I'm pretty sure this will be well received at your next get-together. And good news: If you have any carb-conscious guests, they can just eat the meatballs without the bun. It's a win-win for the entire group!

Pantry Staples: Italian seasoning, garlic salt, ground black pepper, olive oil
Hands-On Time: 10 minutes
Cook Time: 14 minutes

Serves 6

1 pound 80/20 ground beef
2 large eggs, lightly beaten
1 tablespoon Italian seasoning
1 teaspoon garlic salt
½ teaspoon ground black pepper
½ cup panko bread crumbs
3 tablespoons olive oil, divided
1 (24-ounce) jar marinara sauce
1 cup water
6 slider buns

STUFF THOSE MEATBALLS!
Add a welcomed ooey-gooey center to your meatball by stuffing it. When forming the meatballs, press one fresh mini mozzarella ball (*ciliegine*) into the middle of each meatball. Cook as usual per recipe.

1 In a medium bowl, combine beef, eggs, Italian seasoning, garlic salt, pepper, and bread crumbs. Form into twelve meatballs.

2 Press the Sauté button on the Instant Pot® and heat 2 tablespoons oil. Place six meatballs around the edge of the pot. Sear all sides of the meatballs for a total of 3–4 minutes. Remove meatballs from the Instant Pot® and set aside. Add remaining 1 tablespoon oil and sear remaining meatballs 3–4 minutes. Remove meatballs from pot and set aside. Press the Cancel button.

3 Discard extra juice and oil. Add seared meatballs to a 7-cup glass baking dish. Add marinara sauce.

4 Add water to the Instant Pot® and insert steam rack. Place glass baking dish on top of steam rack. Lock lid.

5 Press the Manual or Pressure Cook button and adjust time to 6 minutes. When timer beeps, let pressure release naturally for 5 minutes. Quick-release any additional pressure until float valve drops. Unlock lid.

6 Transfer two meatballs and sauce to each slider bun. Serve warm.

PER SERVING:

CALORIES: 358 | FAT: 17g | PROTEIN: 20g | SODIUM: 994mg | FIBER: 3g | CARBOHYDRATES: 26g | NET CARBS: 23g | SUGAR: 8g

Classic Buffalo Chicken Wings

These wings have been a classic for years, and for good reason—they are delicious and very easy to make. Serve with celery and carrot sticks along with your favorite dressing, whether it is blue cheese or ranch! As far as the hot sauce, Frank's RedHot sauce is the kitchen favorite!

Pantry Staples: olive oil, salt, ground black pepper, hot sauce
Hands-On Time: 10 minutes
Cook Time: 10 minutes

Serves 6

2 pounds chicken wings
1 tablespoon olive oil
1 teaspoon salt
½ teaspoon ground black pepper
1 cup water
3 tablespoons unsalted butter, diced
¼ cup hot sauce

1 If you buy chicken wings that are connected, cut them at the joints to separate. Season chicken with oil, salt, and pepper.

2 Add water to the Instant Pot® and insert steamer basket. Add chicken wings to basket. Stand wings up if necessary so as to not overcrowd them. Lock lid.

3 Press the Manual or Pressure Cook button and adjust time to 10 minutes. When timer beeps, let pressure release naturally for 5 minutes. Quick-release any additional pressure until float valve drops. Unlock lid. (For a crisp skin, place wings on a baking sheet and broil 5 minutes.)

4 In a large bowl, add butter and hot sauce. Toss chicken in sauce until butter is melted and wings are coated. Serve warm.

PER SERVING:

CALORIES: 378 | FAT: 27g | PROTEIN: 29g | SODIUM: 813mg | FIBER: 0g | CARBOHYDRATES: 0g | NET CARBS: 0g | SUGAR: 0g

Shanghai Chicken Wings

Add these wings to your very own pupu platter...or just add them to your mouth. In just 20 minutes and with only 5 ingredients, you will have a dish that will delight your taste buds and your busy schedule! Sriracha or gochujang are the recommended hot sauces in this recipe; however, any heat is better than no heat in the balance of this sauce.

Pantry Staples: none
Hands-On Time: 10 minutes
Cook Time: 10 minutes

Serves 6

2 tablespoons honey
¼ cup hoisin sauce
1 tablespoon sriracha
2 pounds chicken wings
2 tablespoons Chinese five-spice powder
1 cup water

ADD IT IN!

Add more depth to this wing sauce by adding a tablespoon of soy sauce and/or a teaspoon of grated fresh ginger.

1   In a large bowl, whisk together honey, hoisin sauce, and sriracha. Set aside.

2   If you buy chicken wings that are connected, cut them at the joint to separate. Season chicken with five-spice powder.

3   Add water to the Instant Pot® and insert steamer basket. Add chicken wings to basket. Stand wings up if necessary so as to not overcrowd them. Lock lid.

4   Press the Manual or Pressure Cook button and adjust time to 10 minutes. When timer beeps, let pressure release naturally for 5 minutes. Quick-release any additional pressure until float valve drops. Unlock lid. (At this point, if you prefer a crispier skin, you can place wings on a baking sheet and broil 5 minutes.)

5   Toss chicken in bowl with sauce. Serve warm.

PER SERVING:

CALORIES: 359 | **FAT:** 20g | **PROTEIN:** 29g | **SODIUM:** 340mg | **FIBER:** 1g | **CARBOHYDRATES:** 12g | **NET CARBS:** 11g | **SUGAR:** 9g

Sparerib Nachos

These tender spareribs elevate your nacho game with few ingredients and not a lot of cooking time. Let your Instant Pot® do the work without having to heat the house with low and slow cooking. The happy mouths around the nacho tray will be proof enough!

Pantry Staples: beef broth
Hands-On Time: 15 minutes
Cook Time: 40 minutes

Serves 8

- 3 pounds pork spareribs, cut into 2-rib sections
- 2 cups beef broth
- 1 (1-ounce) packet taco seasoning mix
- 1 (18-ounce) bag tortilla chips
- 2 cups shredded Cheddar cheese
- 3 medium Roma tomatoes, diced

LOAD 'EM UP!

Personalize these nachos for yourself or for your crowd. Additional toppings can be used on these nachos: sour cream, guacamole, fresh cilantro, diced avocado, sliced black olives, jalapeños, and refried beans.

1 Add ribs, broth, and taco seasoning to the Instant Pot®. Lock lid.

2 Press the Manual or Pressure Cook button and adjust time to 40 minutes. When timer beeps, let pressure release naturally for 10 minutes. Quick-release any additional pressure until float valve drops. Unlock lid. When cool enough to handle, use two forks to shred pork off of bones. Discard bones.

3 Scatter chips on a serving platter. Using a slotted spoon, place rib meat over chips. Add cheese and tomatoes. Serve immediately.

PER SERVING:

CALORIES: 702 | FAT: 40g | PROTEIN: 31g | SODIUM: 528mg | FIBER: 3g | CARBOHYDRATES: 45g | NET CARBS: 42g | SUGAR: 2g

Warm Shrimp Dip

This dip is so easy to make and divinely delicious, especially served on sliced French bread. However, chips, vegetables, and crackers are perfectly acceptable! Your favorite hot sauce will work in this recipe.

Pantry Staples: hot sauce, salt, ground black pepper
Hands-On Time: 10 minutes
Cook Time: 13 minutes

Serves 6

Zest and juice of ¼ large lemon
8 ounces cream cheese, softened
¾ pound cooked peeled and deveined shrimp, diced
2 teaspoons hot sauce
2 medium green onions, thinly sliced (whites and greens separated)
1 teaspoon salt
¼ teaspoon ground black pepper
1 cup water
¼ cup grated Parmesan cheese

1 In a medium bowl, combine lemon juice and zest, cream cheese, shrimp, hot sauce, onion whites, salt, and pepper. Transfer to a 7-cup glass bowl.

2 Preheat oven to broiler at 500°F.

3 Add water to the Instant Pot® and insert steam rack. Place glass bowl on steam rack. Lock lid.

4 Press the Manual or Pressure Cook button and adjust time to 8 minutes. When timer beeps, quick-release pressure until float valve drops. Unlock lid. Sprinkle cheese on top.

5 Place dip under broiler 5 minutes to brown cheese. Garnish with onion greens. Serve warm.

PER SERVING:

CALORIES: 205 | FAT: 12g | PROTEIN: 17g | SODIUM: 715mg | FIBER: 0g | CARBOHYDRATES: 3g | NET CARBS: 3g | SUGAR: 1g

Creamy Avocado Salsa Verde

The avocados in this recipe not only add a creamy texture to the slightly fruity and tart flavor of a traditional salsa verde; they also add a cooling element to this fresh and easy mix.

Pantry Staples: salt
Hands-On Time: 10 minutes
Cook Time: 2 minutes

Serves 8

1 pound tomatillos (about 8), outer husks removed
1 medium serrano chile, seeded
½ cup chopped fresh cilantro
2 teaspoons salt
2 medium ripe avocados, peeled, pitted, and diced
Juice of 1 medium lime
½ cup water

1 Place tomatillos in the Instant Pot®. Add enough water to cover tomatillos. Lock lid.

2 Press the Manual or Pressure Cook button and adjust time to 2 minutes. When timer beeps, let pressure release naturally until float valve drops. Unlock lid.

3 Drain the Instant Pot®. To a food processor or blender, add tomatillos, serrano chile, cilantro, salt, avocados, lime juice, and water. Pulse until well combined, about 1–2 minutes.

4 Transfer to a serving dish, cover, and chill before serving.

PER SERVING:

CALORIES: 75 | **FAT:** 5g | **PROTEIN:** 1g | **SODIUM:** 584mg | **FIBER:** 3g | **CARBOHYDRATES:** 7g | **NET CARBS:** 4g | **SUGAR:** 2g

Happy Dip

It's a good thing this recipe is quick to make, because it's so delicious it will be gone in seconds! Serve this absolutely addictive dip with toasted French bread slices, butter crackers, or a vegetable tray.

Pantry Staples: Italian seasoning
Hands-On Time: 10 minutes
Cook Time: 3 minutes

Serves 8

8 ounces cream cheese, softened

1 tablespoon Italian seasoning

6 slices bacon, cooked and crumbled

2 cups shredded sharp Cheddar cheese

16 ounces sour cream

1 medium green onion, sliced (whites and greens separated)

1 cup water

CHANGE IT UP!

Replace the Italian seasoning with a 1-ounce packet of dry ranch salad dressing mix for a slightly different flavor. If you want a little kick, add ¼ cup chopped jarred jalapeños to the mixture.

1 In a medium bowl, combine cream cheese, Italian seasoning, bacon, Cheddar cheese, sour cream, and onion whites. Transfer mixture to a 7-cup glass bowl.

2 Add water to the Instant Pot® and insert steam rack. Place glass bowl on steam rack. Lock lid.

3 Press the Manual or Pressure Cook button and adjust time to 3 minutes. When timer beeps, quick-release pressure until float valve drops. Unlock lid.

4 Remove glass baking dish from pot. Garnish with onion greens. Serve warm.

PER SERVING:

CALORIES: 361 | FAT: 29g | PROTEIN: 13g | SODIUM: 457mg | FIBER: 0g | CARBOHYDRATES: 3g | NET CARBS: 3g | SUGAR: 3g

Pizza-Style Stuffed Mushrooms

What better duo can you imagine than pizza plus mushrooms? Delicious and super easy to create, this addictive twosome needs to be in your life!

Pantry Staples: none
Hands-On Time: 10 minutes
Cook Time: 2 minutes

Serves 4

¼ cup jarred pizza sauce
8 ounces whole baby bella mushrooms (approximately 10), stems removed
½ cup shredded mozzarella
¼ cup small-diced pepperoni
1 cup water
5 fresh basil leaves, julienned

ADD IT IN!

This is where your imagination and taste buds can go wild. If pepperoni isn't your thing, add bell peppers, olives, sausage, bacon, onions, or whatever you want! Or make a variety of toppings if you are feeding a group.

1 Spoon pizza sauce evenly into mushroom caps to cover bottoms. Top with mozzarella cheese and then pepperoni.

2 Pour water into the Instant Pot®. Place stuffed mushrooms in steamer basket, then insert basket in pot. Lock lid.

3 Press the Manual or Pressure Cook button and adjust time to 2 minutes. Adjust pressure to Low. When timer beeps, quick-release pressure until float valve drops. Unlock lid.

4 Transfer mushrooms to a serving dish. Garnish with basil. Serve warm.

PER SERVING:

CALORIES: 98 | FAT: 6g | PROTEIN: 7g | SODIUM: 276mg | FIBER: 1g | CARBOHYDRATES: 5g | NET CARBS: 4g | SUGAR: 2g

South of the Border Tri-Bean Dip

This dip is delicious just as it is, but if you'd like to make it even better, garnish it with sour cream and fresh cilantro. Serve it up with cut vegetables or tortilla chips and you have a party! I recommend using Tabasco brand hot sauce for this recipe.

Pantry Staples: chicken broth, hot sauce, salt
Hands-On Time: 10 minutes
Cook Time: 7 minutes

Serves 6

2 (15-ounce) cans tri-bean blend (kidney, pinto, and black beans), drained and rinsed
¼ cup chicken broth
2 teaspoons hot sauce
1 small red onion, peeled and diced
2 teaspoons chili powder
1 teaspoon salt
1 (4-ounce) can diced green chiles, including juice
1 (14.5-ounce) can fire-roasted diced tomatoes, including juice

1   Place all ingredients in the Instant Pot® and stir to combine. Lock lid.

2   Press the Manual or Pressure Cook button and adjust time to 7 minutes. When timer beeps, let pressure release naturally until float valve drops. Unlock lid.

3   Use an immersion blender to blend dip in pot until smooth, or use a stand blender to blend dip in batches.

4   Transfer dip to a dish. Serve warm.

PER SERVING:

CALORIES: 146 | FAT: 0g | PROTEIN: 9g | SODIUM: 789mg | FIBER: 8g | CARBOHYDRATES: 28g | NET CARBS: 20g | SUGAR: 3g

Kalamata Olive Hummus

This twist on a traditional Middle Eastern hummus lends a saltiness and Greek nod. The olives give not only a briny addition but also a deep color.

Pantry Staples: garlic salt, olive oil
Hands-On Time: 10 minutes
Cook Time: 30 minutes

Serves 6

½ cup dried chickpeas
2 cups water
¾ cup chopped Kalamata olives, divided
1 tablespoon tahini
Juice and zest of 1 small lemon
¼ teaspoon ground cumin
¼ teaspoon garlic salt
2 tablespoons olive oil plus a drizzle for garnish

WHAT IS TAHINI AND HOW DO YOU MAKE IT?

Also known as *Ardeh*, tahini is a Middle Eastern paste made from ground toasted sesame seeds. Used in dishes such as hummus and baba ghanoush, it can be found in most supermarkets. To make your own quick tahini, pulse 1 cup toasted sesame seeds in a food processor along with 3 tablespoons olive oil, slowly pulsing in 1 tablespoon oil at a time until a thin paste forms. Add ⅛ teaspoon of salt, if desired.

1 Add chickpeas and water to the Instant Pot®. Lock lid. Press the Bean button and cook for the default time of 30 minutes. When timer beeps, let pressure release naturally for 5 minutes. Quick-release any additional pressure until float valve drops. Unlock lid.

2 Drain pot, reserving water in a small bowl.

3 Transfer chickpeas from pot into a food processor or stand blender. Add olives (all but 1 tablespoon reserved for garnish), tahini, lemon juice and zest, cumin, garlic salt, and oil. If consistency is too thick, slowly add reserved water, 1 tablespoon at a time. You are looking for a loose paste consistency.

4 Transfer hummus to a serving dish. Garnish with remaining olives and a drizzle of oil. Serve.

PER SERVING:

CALORIES: 153 | FAT: 10g | PROTEIN: 4g | SODIUM: 317mg | FIBER: 2g | CARBOHYDRATES: 12g | NET CARBS: 10g | SUGAR: 2g

Sausage-Stuffed Mushrooms

These delicious stuffed mushrooms are great as a snack, a side, or an appetizer for guests. But don't throw away those stems! Mushroom stems, which are usually discarded, are ideal additions to breakfast scrambles, omelets, sauces, homemade broth, and even those super healthy green smoothies!

Pantry Staples: olive oil, garlic salt, ground black pepper
Hands-On Time: 10 minutes
Cook Time: 7 minutes

Serves 4

- 1 tablespoon olive oil
- ¼ pound ground pork sausage
- 1 tablespoon grated yellow onion
- 1 tablespoon gluten-free bread crumbs
- 2 tablespoons cream cheese, softened
- ¼ teaspoon garlic salt
- ¼ teaspoon ground black pepper
- 1 cup water
- 8 ounces whole baby bella mushrooms (approximately 10), stems removed

1 Press the Sauté button on the Instant Pot® and heat oil. Add sausage and onion to pot. Stir-fry 5 minutes until sausage is no longer pink. Press the Cancel button.

2 Transfer mixture to a medium bowl and use paper towels to dab off excess oil and fat. Add bread crumbs, cream cheese, garlic salt, and pepper. Stir to combine.

3 Pour water into the Instant Pot®. Stuff an equal amount of mixture into each mushroom cap and place caps in steamer basket. Insert basket in pot. Lock lid.

4 Press the Manual or Pressure Cook button and adjust time to 2 minutes. Adjust pressure to Low. When timer beeps, quick-release pressure until float valve drops. Unlock lid.

5 Transfer mushrooms to a serving dish. Serve warm.

PER SERVING:

CALORIES: 145 | FAT: 10g | PROTEIN: 8g | SODIUM: 188mg | FIBER: 1g | CARBOHYDRATES: 5g | NET CARBS: 4g | SUGAR: 1g

BBQ Pork Sliders

When you think of cooking a pork shoulder, you probably think about cooking it low and slow for 6–8 hours. With the Instant Pot®, the same result can be achieved in a significantly reduced amount of time. Enjoy these sliders with coleslaw, sliced pickles, mustard, or whatever your heart desires. Also, have fun choosing your barbecue sauce. Are you feeling a little molasses sweet or red pepper hot? There are so many varieties to choose from depending on your mood and your guests.

Pantry Staples: salt, ground black pepper, olive oil
Hands-On Time: 15 minutes
Cook Time: 60 minutes

Serves 10

1 (3-pound) pork shoulder
2 teaspoons salt
2 teaspoons ground black pepper
2 tablespoons olive oil
1 cup barbecue sauce
20 slider buns

1 Season pork shoulder with salt and pepper.

2 Press the Sauté button on the Instant Pot® and heat oil. Sear pork shoulder on all sides, ensuring they are browned, a total of 8–10 minutes. Add enough water (2–3 cups) to almost cover meat. Press the Cancel button. Lock lid.

3 Press the Manual or Pressure Cook button and adjust time to 45 minutes. When timer beeps, let pressure release naturally for 10 minutes. Quick-release any additional pressure until float valve drops. Press the Cancel button. Unlock lid.

4 Transfer pork to a platter. Using two forks, shred meat. Discard all but 2 tablespoons cooking liquid. Add pork, 2 tablespoons cooking liquid, and barbecue sauce back into the Instant Pot®. Press the Sauté button and stir-fry meat 4–5 minutes, creating some crispy edges.

5 Serve warm on buns.

PER SERVING:

CALORIES: 394 | FAT: 10g | PROTEIN: 29g | SODIUM: 1,129mg | FIBER: 2g | CARBOHYDRATES: 48g | NET CARBS: 46g | SUGAR: 16g

Steamed Artichokes with Lemon-Garlic Yogurt Sauce

If you are having a get-together or want to introduce your friends to a new appetizer, steam some of these artichokes. Artichokes are fairly inexpensive and easy to fix, and they make a fun appetizer to gather around for good food and conversation.

Pantry Staples: salt
Hands-On Time: 15 minutes
Cook Time: 5 minutes

Serves 6

Yogurt Sauce
¼ cup plain Greek yogurt
Juice and zest of ½ medium lemon
3 cloves garlic, peeled and minced
1 tablespoon Dijon mustard
⅛ teaspoon salt

Steamed Artichokes
6 medium artichokes
1 cup water
1 teaspoon salt

HOW TO EAT AN ARTICHOKE

So, you are at a party and a beautifully steamed artichoke is presented. How on earth do you eat it? Simply pull off a leaf, dip the end into the prepared sauce, and pull the pulp on the end of the leaf through your teeth. Discard the used leaf. That's it!

1   In a small bowl, whisk together yogurt sauce ingredients. Refrigerate until ready to use.

2   Clean artichokes by clipping off the top third of the leaves and removing the tougher exterior leaves. Trim bottoms so that they have a flat surface.

3   Add water to the Instant Pot® and insert steam rack. Place artichokes upright in a steamer basket and lower basket onto steam rack. Sprinkle artichokes with 1 teaspoon salt. Lock lid.

4   Press the Manual or Pressure Cook button and adjust time to 5 minutes. When timer beeps, quick-release pressure until float valve drops. Unlock lid.

5   Lift artichokes very carefully out of pot (they will be so tender that they may fall apart), transfer to a large plate, and serve with yogurt sauce for dipping.

PER SERVING:

CALORIES: 92 | FAT: 1g | PROTEIN: 6g | SODIUM: 1,366mg | FIBER: 8g | CARBOHYDRATES: 17g | NET CARBS: 9g | SUGAR: 2g

Mini Reuben Potato Skins

That deli-delicious Reuben is reimagined in tasty potato skins. You'll find that the salty corned beef (or pastrami, if you prefer to use that instead) mixes so well with the creamy potatoes, you may never go back to bread on your Reuben again!

Pantry Staples: olive oil, beef broth, salt
Hands-On Time: 15 minutes
Cook Time: 22 minutes

Serves 10

2 pounds (about 10) red potatoes
4 tablespoons olive oil, divided
1 cup beef broth
½ teaspoon salt
2 cups shredded Swiss cheese
½ cup chopped corned beef
½ cup sauerkraut
2 tablespoons Russian dressing

LEFTOVER POTATOES?

Don't throw away the leftover cooked potatoes. There are so many ways to use them. Either mash them for later or add them to any meatloaf recipe. Even better, make potato cakes. Just add some salt, pepper, an egg, and maybe a little cheese, and you can quick-fry some patties on your stovetop to accompany almost any dish!

1   Use a fork to pierce each potato three or four times. Press the Sauté button on the Instant Pot® and heat 3 tablespoons oil. Add potatoes. Coat all sides of potatoes with oil and sauté about 4–5 minutes until browned. Add broth. Press the Cancel button. Lock lid.

2   Press the Manual or Pressure Cook button and adjust time to 7 minutes. When timer beeps, quick-release pressure until float valve drops. Unlock lid.

3   Let potatoes cool until you can handle them, then discard liquid.

4   Preheat oven to 350°F. Line a baking sheet with parchment paper.

5   Cut potatoes in half lengthwise. Scoop out approximately half of each potato, creating a boat. Brush potatoes with remaining oil. Place boats on prepared baking sheet. Season with salt. Bake 5 minutes.

6   Distribute cheese among potato halves. Top with corned beef. Bake potato skins for an additional 5 minutes until cheese is melted.

7   Remove from oven and top each skin with equal amounts sauerkraut. Drizzle with Russian dressing. Serve warm.

PER SERVING:

CALORIES: 200 | FAT: 13g | PROTEIN: 9g | SODIUM: 380mg | FIBER: 1g | CARBOHYDRATES: 11g | NET CARBS: 10g | SUGAR: 2g

Cajun Boiled Peanuts

If you've never had boiled peanuts, then you should know they aren't rotten. Some people actually like their peanuts boiled and soft. Give 'em a chance. They may be an acquired taste, but open your mind, as these are enjoyed by so many in the South and around the world.

Pantry Staples: salt
Hands-On Time: 5 minutes
Cook Time: 55 minutes

Serves 8

1 pound raw, unsalted peanuts, rinsed
6 cups water
¼ cup Cajun seasoning
1 tablespoon cayenne seasoning
¼ cup salt

BROWN BAG IT!

Consider serving your guests their portion of boiled peanuts in a brown paper lunch bag. It's how you receive them on the roadside, so why not add some kitschy flair to your own party?

1 Place all ingredients in the Instant Pot®. Lock lid.

2 Press the Manual or Pressure Cook button and adjust time to 55 minutes. When timer beeps, let pressure release naturally for 10 minutes. Quick-release any additional pressure until float valve drops. Unlock lid.

3 Strain liquid and transfer peanuts to a serving dish with an additional bowl for the shells. Serve.

PER SERVING:

CALORIES: 180 | FAT: 12g | PROTEIN: 8g | SODIUM: 461mg | FIBER: 5g | CARBOHYDRATES: 12g | NET CARBS: 7g | SUGAR: 1g

6

Side Dishes

Side dishes sometimes take a back seat to our full schedule, especially on busy nights. And, unfortunately, that usually means our vegetables are kicked to the side. With the Instant Pot®, you can have flavorfully seasoned vegetables in minutes while the main dish is being prepared. In addition, pressure cooking vegetables in your Instant Pot® retains more nutrients than boiling them on the stovetop or roasting them in the oven.

From simple vegetables to chilled salads, this chapter has got you covered with a myriad of delicious side dish recipes, including Avocado Corn Salad, Loaded Broccoli, and Down-Home Rainbow Chard. And once you get comfortable with some of the basics, you should feel free to get creative and make some of your own masterpieces.

Garlic-Buttery Button Mushrooms

Mushrooms are excellent, but cooked down with beautiful flavors? Amazing!

Pantry Staples: beef broth
Hands-On Time: 5 minutes
Cook Time: 28 minutes

Serves 8

½ cup unsalted butter

6 cloves garlic, peeled and diced

32 ounces whole button mushrooms

1 cup dry white wine

3 cups beef broth

¼ cup chopped fresh parsley

1 Press the Sauté button on the Instant Pot®. Add butter and heat until melted. Add garlic and mushrooms and toss to coat with butter. Stir-fry 3 minutes until mushrooms start to get tender. Add wine and broth. Press the Cancel button. Lock lid.

2 Press the Manual or Pressure Cook button and adjust time to 25 minutes. When timer beeps, let pressure release naturally until float valve drops. Unlock lid. Stir in parsley.

3 Using a slotted spoon, transfer mushrooms to a serving bowl. Serve warm.

PER SERVING:

CALORIES: 55 | FAT: 3g | PROTEIN: 4g | SODIUM: 106mg | FIBER: 1g | CARBOHYDRATES: 4g | NET CARBS: 3g | SUGAR: 2g

Picnic Deviled Eggs

Are you off to grill with friends and family and they expect you to bring a side dish? Deviled eggs should be your go-to. They are super easy to create and absolutely delicious. This traditional side pretty much fits into most folks' dietary restrictions, so hold your head up and deliver these delicacies with pride.

Pantry Staples: salt, ground black pepper
Hands-On Time: 15 minutes
Cook Time: 4 minutes

Serves 6

1 cup water
6 large eggs
3 tablespoons mayonnaise
1 teaspoon yellow mustard
1 teaspoon finely diced dill pickles plus ⅛ teaspoon pickle juice
⅛ teaspoon salt
⅛ teaspoon ground black pepper
⅛ teaspoon smoked paprika

YOLK HACK!

When making deviled eggs, cook seven eggs instead of six...or thirteen instead of twelve. There are two reasons why. One, there is usually an egg that doesn't want to peel "pretty," so the white can go straight in your mouth. Save that yolk. Two, even if all of the eggs peel pretty, having an extra yolk adds bulk to the beautiful filling. That extra yolk takes you to filling nirvana.

1. Add water to the Instant Pot® and insert steamer basket. Place eggs in basket. Lock lid.

2. Press the Manual or Pressure Cook button and adjust time to 4 minutes. When timer beeps, quick-release pressure until float valve drops. Unlock lid.

3. Create an ice bath by adding 1 cup ice and 1 cup water to a medium bowl. Transfer eggs to ice bath to stop the cooking process.

4. Peel eggs. Slice each egg in half lengthwise and place yolks in a small bowl. Place egg white halves on a serving tray.

5. Add mayonnaise, mustard, pickles, pickle juice, salt, and pepper to small bowl with yolks. Use a fork to blend until smooth.

6. Spoon yolk filling into egg white halves. Garnish with paprika. Serve chilled.

PER SERVING:

CALORIES: 124 | **FAT:** 9g | **PROTEIN:** 6g | **SODIUM:** 168mg | **FIBER:** 0g | **CARBOHYDRATES:** 1g | **NET CARBS:** 1g | **SUGAR:** 1g

Autumnal Acorn Squash

When it's that time of the year when all of the weird fall squash start making their way into the produce section, buy them! You won't regret the richness and comfort of these gourds when making this dish.

Pantry Staples: salt
Hands-On Time: 10 minutes
Cook Time: 7 minutes

Serves 2

1 medium acorn squash, halved and seeded
4 teaspoons unsalted butter, cut into 4 pats
2 tablespoons packed dark brown sugar
¼ teaspoon ground cinnamon
⅛ teaspoon salt
2 cups water

1 Using a paring knife, make ¼" crosshatch pattern on flesh of squash.

2 Add butter, brown sugar, cinnamon, and salt to each squash half.

3 Add water to the Instant Pot® and insert steamer basket. Arrange squash in basket. Lock lid.

4 Press the Manual or Pressure Cook button and adjust time to 7 minutes. When timer beeps, let pressure release naturally for 5 minutes. Quick-release any additional pressure until float valve drops. Unlock lid.

5 Transfer squash to two dishes. Serve warm.

PER SERVING:

CALORIES: 206 | FAT: 7g | PROTEIN: 2g | SODIUM: 155mg | FIBER: 3g | CARBOHYDRATES: 36g | NET CARBS: 33g | SUGAR: 13g

Jalapeño-Cheddar Hush Puppies

Are you having a fish fry? Hush puppies are always welcome to the table. Generally, you'd need a deep fryer, but with your Instant Pot® you have a quick and cool way to achieve hush puppy happiness.

Pantry Staples: none
Hands-On Time: 10 minutes
Cook Time: 28 minutes

Serves 4

1 (8-ounce) packet Martha White Hush Puppy Mix With Onion Flavor
¾ cup whole milk
¼ cup finely shredded Cheddar cheese
2 tablespoons grated yellow onion
1 large jalapeño, seeded and diced
1 cup water

1 Grease a seven-hole silicone egg mold.

2 In a medium bowl, combine hush puppy mix and milk. Add cheese, onion, and jalapeño and stir to combine. Fill egg mold with half of batter. Cover egg mold with aluminum foil.

3 Add water to the Instant Pot® and insert steam rack. Place filled egg mold on steam rack. Lock lid.

4 Press the Manual or Pressure Cook button and adjust time to 14 minutes. When timer beeps, quick-release pressure until float valve drops. Unlock lid.

5 Allow hush puppies to cool for 5 minutes, pop out of mold, and then transfer to a cooling rack. Repeat with remaining batter.

6 Serve warm.

PER SERVING:

CALORIES: 248 | **FAT:** 4g | **PROTEIN:** 8g | **SODIUM:** 1,025mg | **FIBER:** 3g | **CARBOHYDRATES:** 44g | **NET CARBS:** 41g | **SUGAR:** 6g

Twice-Baked Potatoes

Traditional twice-baked potatoes are labor- and time-intensive, taking over an hour or more to prepare. But by using your Instant Pot® and only a handful of ingredients, you can get a delicious twice-baked potato with all the salty and cheesy goodness in half the time. Now that is a win-win!

Pantry Staples: salt, ground black pepper
Hands-On Time: 5 minutes
Cook Time: 13 minutes

Serves 4

1 cup water
2 medium russet potatoes
2 slices bacon, cooked and crumbled
¼ cup whole milk
4 tablespoons unsalted butter
½ cup shredded Cheddar cheese, divided
½ teaspoon salt
¼ teaspoon ground black pepper

ADD IT IN!

After you have made these delicious side potatoes, you may want to dress them up a bit. If that is so, add a dollop of sour cream and some chopped fresh chives atop each twice-baked potato.

1 Add water to the Instant Pot® and insert steamer basket. Pierce potatoes with a fork and add to basket. Lock lid.

2 Press the Manual or Pressure Cook button and adjust time to 10 minutes. When timer beeps, let pressure release naturally until float valve drops. Press the Cancel button. Unlock lid.

3 Transfer potatoes to a cutting board and let cool enough to handle.

4 In a medium mixing bowl, add bacon, milk, butter, ¼ cup cheese, salt and pepper.

5 Slice potatoes in half lengthwise. Scoop out potato flesh, leaving a bowl-like shell.

6 Add scooped potatoes to bowl with remaining ingredients. Using a potato masher or the back of a fork, work ingredients together. Distribute mixture evenly among the bowl-like shells. Sprinkle with remaining cheese. Place potatoes in basket and insert in the Instant Pot®. Lock lid.

7 Press the Manual or Pressure Cook button and adjust time to 3 minutes. When timer beeps, let pressure release naturally until float valve drops. Unlock lid. Serve.

PER SERVING:

CALORIES: 275 | **FAT:** 17g | **PROTEIN:** 8g | **SODIUM:** 494mg | **FIBER:** 2g | **CARBOHYDRATES:** 19g | **NET CARBS:** 17g | **SUGAR:** 2g

Steamed Fingerling Potatoes

These potatoes are the perfect side dish for a juicy steak! Also, for the busy home cook, fingerling potatoes are a great addition. There is no need to peel or dice these small tubers: Just give them a good scrub, and they are ready for steamed perfection in just minutes with the Instant Pot®.

Pantry Staples: salt, ground black pepper
Hands-On Time: 5 minutes
Cook Time: 11 minutes

Serves 6

- 1½ pounds fingerling potatoes
- 3 tablespoons unsalted butter, divided
- 4 cloves garlic, peeled and chopped
- 2 cups water
- 1 teaspoon salt
- ½ teaspoon ground black pepper
- 2 tablespoons chopped fresh chives

1 Use a fork to pierce each potato three times.

2 Press the Sauté button on the Instant Pot®. Add 1 tablespoon butter and heat until melted. Add potatoes to pot. Stir-fry 4 minutes. Add garlic and heat an additional 1 minute. Press the Cancel button.

3 Add water to the Instant Pot®. Lock lid.

4 Press the Manual or Pressure Cook button and adjust time to 6 minutes. When timer beeps, quick-release pressure until float valve drops. Unlock lid.

5 Using a slotted spoon, transfer potatoes to a serving dish. Toss with remaining 2 tablespoons butter, salt, and pepper. Garnish with chives. Serve warm.

PER SERVING:

CALORIES: 132 | FAT: 5g | PROTEIN: 2g | SODIUM: 406mg | FIBER: 3g | CARBOHYDRATES: 19g | NET CARBS: 16g | SUGAR: 1g

Jalapeño Popper Potato Salad

Jalapeño poppers have become a commonplace appetizer, but when those flavors are thrown into a traditional dish like potato salad they really give it some new flair. Show up at your family reunion with this ultramodern dish that still hits all the notes of nostalgia!

Pantry Staples: chicken broth, garlic salt, ground black pepper
Hands-On Time: 10 minutes
Cook Time: 5 minutes

Serves 8

- 1 pound (about 5 medium) red potatoes, cut in ½" cubes
- ½ cup chicken broth
- ⅓ cup mayonnaise
- 1 teaspoon garlic salt
- 1 teaspoon ground black pepper
- 6 slices bacon, cooked and crumbled
- 1 cup shredded sharp Cheddar cheese
- 2 small jalapeños, seeded and diced

1 Add potatoes and broth to the Instant Pot®. Lock lid.

2 Press the Manual or Pressure Cook button and adjust time to 5 minutes. When timer beeps, quick-release pressure until float valve drops. Unlock lid.

3 Drain potatoes and set aside.

4 In a large bowl, whisk mayonnaise, garlic salt, and black pepper. Add potatoes, bacon, cheese, and jalapeños. Carefully toss to combine.

5 Refrigerate covered until ready to be served chilled.

PER SERVING:

CALORIES: 201 | FAT: 14g | PROTEIN: 8g | SODIUM: 572mg | FIBER: 1g | CARBOHYDRATES: 10g | NET CARBS: 9g | SUGAR: 1g

Loaded Broccoli

Potatoes aren't the only lucky ones that can be loaded up! Serve your broccoli naysayers this dish and watch them change their minds. This dish is also great for the keto diet!

Pantry Staples: salt
Hands-On Time: 5 minutes
Cook Time: 0 minutes

Serves 4

1 cup water
1 medium head broccoli, chopped
½ teaspoon salt
1 cup shredded sharp Cheddar cheese
⅓ cup sour cream
4 slices bacon, cooked and crumbled
2 tablespoons chopped fresh chives

1　Add water to the Instant Pot® and insert steamer basket. Arrange broccoli in basket in an even layer. Lock lid.

2　Press the Steam button and adjust time to 0 minutes. When timer beeps, quick-release pressure until float valve drops. Unlock lid.

3　Remove steamer basket. Transfer broccoli to a serving dish and season with salt. Top with cheese. Garnish with sour cream, bacon, and chives. Serve.

PER SERVING:

CALORIES: 22 | FAT: 16g | PROTEIN: 13g | SODIUM: 691mg | FIBER: 0g | CARBOHYDRATES: 4g | NET CARBS: 4g | SUGAR: 1g

Cauliflower with Cheese Sauce

Do you have any vegetable scaredy-cats in the house? Throw some melty cheese on those vegetables, and you will be sure to have some fans!

Pantry Staples: all-purpose flour, salt, ground black pepper
Hands-On Time: 5 minutes
Cook Time: 7 minutes

Serves 4

1 cup water
1 large head cauliflower, cut into florets
1 tablespoon unsalted butter
½ cup grated Monterey jack cheese
¾ cup whole milk
1 tablespoon all-purpose flour
⅛ teaspoon ground nutmeg
½ teaspoon salt
½ teaspoon ground black pepper

1 Add water to the Instant Pot® and insert steamer basket. Add cauliflower to basket. Lock lid.

2 Press the Steam button and adjust time to 5 minutes. When timer beeps, quick-release pressure until float valve drops. Press the Cancel button. Unlock lid.

3 Transfer cauliflower to a serving dish and drain pot.

4 Press the Sauté button on the Instant Pot®. Add butter and heat until melted. Add cheese, milk, flour, nutmeg, salt, and pepper. Whisk 2 minutes until smooth.

5 Pour sauce over cauliflower in dish. Serve warm.

PER SERVING:

CALORIES: 165 | FAT: 8g | PROTEIN: 9g | SODIUM: 457mg | FIBER: 4g | CARBOHYDRATES: 14g | NET CARBS: 10g | SUGAR: 6g

Avocado Corn Salad

Corn on the cob is effortlessly cooked in your Instant Pot®, and when added to a salad with these other fresh ingredients, it is a showstopper! This dish should fit the bill of all your guests, and you'll receive lots of "Mmmm" responses!

Pantry Staples: olive oil, salt, ground black pepper
Hands-On Time: 10 minutes
Cook Time: 2 minutes

Serves 6

1½ cups water

3 fresh ears corn, shucked and halved

Juice and zest of 1 medium lime

¼ cup olive oil

¼ teaspoon salt

¼ teaspoon ground black pepper

2 ripe medium avocados, peeled, pitted, and diced

½ cup diced English cucumber

1 cup halved cherry tomatoes

1 Add water and corn to the Instant Pot®. Lock lid.

2 Press the Manual or Pressure Cook button and adjust time to 2 minutes. When timer beeps, quick-release pressure until float valve drops. Unlock lid.

3 Transfer corn to a serving dish and let cool enough to handle. Cut kernels off of cobs.

4 In a large bowl, whisk together lime juice and zest, oil, salt, and pepper. Toss in corn, avocados, cucumber, and tomatoes.

5 Refrigerate covered until ready to be served. Serve chilled.

PER SERVING:

CALORIES: 210 | FAT: 16g | PROTEIN: 3g | SODIUM: 102mg | FIBER: 5g | CARBOHYDRATES: 16g | NET CARBS: 11g | SUGAR: 3g

Mashed Sweet Potatoes

Using the Instant Pot® steam to cook your sweet potatoes really yields a soft tuber. You don't have to go through the trouble to boil water on your stovetop or utilize that microwave; instead you can just place your potatoes in the Instant Pot® and let it take care of all the work for you!

Pantry Staples: salt
Hands-On Time: 10 minutes
Cook Time: 10 minutes

Serves 6

3 pounds sweet potatoes, peeled and diced large
2 cups water
½ teaspoon ground cinnamon
½ teaspoon salt
4 tablespoons unsalted butter, cut into 4 pats
⅓ cup whole milk

1 Add potatoes and water to the Instant Pot®. Lock lid.

2 Press the Manual or Pressure Cook button and adjust time to 10 minutes. When timer beeps, let pressure release naturally until float valve drops. Unlock lid.

3 Drain water from pot. Add cinnamon, salt, and butter to potatoes. Add a little milk at a time until desired consistency is reached. Using an immersion blender directly in the Instant Pot®, cream the sweet potatoes. Serve warm.

PER SERVING:

CALORIES: 231 | FAT: 8g | PROTEIN: 3g | SODIUM: 255mg | FIBER: 5g | CARBOHYDRATES: 37g | NET CARBS: 32g | SUGAR: 12g

Down-Home Rainbow Chard

Most greens have a slight bitter note to them, but as most southern chefs know, adding a little vinegar, sugar, and hot sauce really balances out that flavor, making this a dish you crave. Whether you use rainbow chard, mustard greens, or turnip greens, add this deeply nutritional dish to your weekly routine. It's excellent served with a ham slice, some corn bread, and a spoonful of chow-chow.

Pantry Staples: hot sauce, chicken broth, granulated sugar, salt, ground black pepper
Hands-On Time: 15 minutes
Cook Time: 8 minutes

Serves 6

- 2 bunches rainbow chard, chopped (spines removed)
- 1 small yellow onion, peeled and diced
- ¼ cup apple cider vinegar
- 1 teaspoon hot sauce
- 1 smoked ham hock
- 1 cup chicken broth
- ½ teaspoon granulated sugar
- ½ teaspoon salt
- ¼ teaspoon ground black pepper

1 Place all ingredients in the Instant Pot®. Lock lid.

2 Press the Manual or Pressure Cook button and adjust time to 8 minutes. When timer beeps, let pressure release naturally until float valve drops. Unlock lid.

3 Flake off ham from bone and discard bone. Stir to incorporate ingredients.

4 Transfer to a serving dish and serve warm.

PER SERVING:

CALORIES: 215 | FAT: 15g | PROTEIN: 14g | SODIUM: 1,608mg | FIBER: 4g | CARBOHYDRATES: 9g | NET CARBS: 5g | SUGAR: 3g

Steamed Asparagus with Lemon Aioli

This elegant side dish is amazing served alongside a salmon dish, baked chicken, or even a grilled steak. The earthy, almost slightly bitter asparagus is tamed by the lemon aioli and pairs well with most proteins.

Pantry Staples: salt, ground black pepper
Hands-On Time: 5 minutes
Cook Time: 1 minute

Serves 4

Lemon Aioli
⅓ cup mayonnaise
Zest and juice from ½ medium lemon
2 cloves garlic, peeled and minced
⅛ teaspoon salt

Asparagus
1 cup water
1 pound asparagus spears, woody ends trimmed and discarded
½ teaspoon salt
¼ teaspoon ground black pepper

1 In a small bowl, combine lemon aioli ingredients and refrigerate until ready to use.

2 Add water to the Instant Pot® and insert steamer basket. Place asparagus evenly in basket. Lock lid.

3 Press the Manual or Pressure Cook button and adjust time to 1 minute. Quick-release pressure until float valve drops. Unlock lid.

4 Transfer asparagus to a serving dish and season with salt and pepper. Drizzle with lemon aioli. Serve warm.

PER SERVING:

CALORIES: 140 | FAT: 14g | PROTEIN: 2g | SODIUM: 480mg | FIBER: 1g | CARBOHYDRATES: 4g | NET CARBS: 3g | SUGAR: 1g

Italian-Style Mustard Greens

These mustard greens are taken up a level with the red wine vinegar and red pepper flakes. That acid flavor is then balanced out with the salty flavor of bacon. Swiss chard, turnip greens, and kale can all be substituted in this recipe, or you can use a blend of your favorites. Just be sure to give these leaves a good cleaning and cut out those tough spines before cooking.

Pantry Staples: chicken broth, Italian seasoning, salt, ground black pepper
Hands-On Time: 10 minutes
Cook Time: 10 minutes

Serves 6

2 pounds mustard greens, chopped (spines removed)
1 small sweet onion, peeled and diced
1 cup chicken broth
¼ cup red wine vinegar
⅛ teaspoon red pepper flakes
2 teaspoons Italian seasoning
1 slice bacon
½ teaspoon salt
¼ teaspoon ground black pepper

1 Place all ingredients in the Instant Pot®. Lock lid.

2 Press the Manual or Pressure Cook button and adjust time to 10 minutes. When timer beeps, let pressure release naturally until float valve drops. Unlock lid. Discard bacon.

3 Using a slotted spoon, transfer mustard greens to a serving dish. Serve warm.

PER SERVING:

CALORIES: 38 | FAT: 0.3g | PROTEIN: 4g | SODIUM: 99mg | FIBER: 4g | CARBOHYDRATES: 7g | NET CARBS: 3g | SUGAR: 2g

Mashed Sweet Potatoes and Carrots

This combo is a beta-carotene explosion. In addition, both carrots and sweet potatoes are high in potassium and vitamin A. The sweetness of the potatoes tamp down the sometimes bitter note carrots can have. They work beautifully together, harmoniously balancing each other out.

Pantry Staples: olive oil, vegetable broth, garlic salt
Hands-On Time: 10 minutes
Cook Time: 9 minutes

Serves 6

2 tablespoons olive oil, divided
2 small sweet potatoes, peeled and diced
4 large carrots, peeled and cut into 2″ pieces
2 cups vegetable broth
1 teaspoon garlic salt
¼ teaspoon ground nutmeg
¼ teaspoon ground ginger
2 tablespoons almond milk

1 Press the Sauté button on the Instant Pot® and heat 1 tablespoon oil. Toss sweet potatoes and carrots in oil 1 minute. Add broth. Press the Cancel button. Lock lid.

2 Press the Manual button and adjust time to 8 minutes. When timer beeps, quick-release pressure until float valve drops. Unlock lid.

3 Drain vegetables, reserving liquid.

4 Add 1 tablespoon reserved liquid plus remaining ingredients to vegetables in pot. Use an immersion blender to blend until desired smoothness is reached. If mixture is too thick, add more liquid 1 tablespoon at a time. Serve warm.

PER SERVING:

CALORIES: 85 | FAT: 3g | PROTEIN: 1g | SODIUM: 113mg | FIBER: 2g | CARBOHYDRATES: 13g | NET CARBS: 11g | SUGAR: 5g

Ramen Eggs

These Ramen Eggs will have a nice jammy center. If you prefer harder yolks, add a couple of minutes to the cooking time. Remember, this is your meal. So if you don't have garlic but do have a knob of ginger hanging out, substitute that. Do you have any star anise hiding in the back of your spice rack? Go ahead; add it.

Pantry Staples: none
Hands-On Time: 15 minutes
Cook Time: 6 minutes

Serves 6

Marinade
¼ cup soy sauce (dark soy sauce if you can find it)
¼ cup mirin
2 tablespoons packed light brown sugar
2 cloves garlic, peeled and quartered
½ cup water

Eggs
1 cup water
6 large eggs

WHAT IS MIRIN?

Mirin is an essential Japanese condiment, similar to sake, but sweeter and with a lower alcohol content. It is basically a fermented rice liquor that is used to balance certain dishes. It can be replaced with other vinegars, although they won't deliver the same umami punch as found with mirin.

1 Combine marinade ingredients in a small saucepan. Bring marinade to a simmer over low heat long enough to melt sugar, approximately 2–3 minutes. Remove from heat and let cool to room temperature. Transfer marinade to a medium bowl.

2 Add 1 cup water to the Instant Pot® and insert steamer basket. Add eggs to basket. Lock lid.

3 Press the Manual or Pressure Cook button and adjust time to 3 minutes. When timer beeps, quick-release pressure until float valve drops. Unlock lid.

4 Create an ice bath by adding 1 cup ice and 1 cup water to a medium bowl. Transfer eggs to ice bath to stop the cooking process.

5 Peel cooled eggs and add to bowl with marinade; cover and refrigerate overnight. Cut eggs in half lengthwise. Serve chilled.

PER SERVING:

CALORIES: 95 | **FAT:** 4g | **PROTEIN:** 7g | **SODIUM:** 470mg | **FIBER:** 0g | **CARBOHYDRATES:** 5g | **NET CARBS:** 5g | **SUGAR:** 5g

Milk-Boiled Corn on the Cob

If you have never cooked corn on the cob in milk, then you are missing out. This method enhances the natural milkiness of corn and makes it even more tender. And salt and butter are the best accents to let the corn goodness shine.

Pantry Staples: salt
Hands-On Time: 5 minutes
Cook Time: 2 minutes

Serves 8

1 cup whole milk

½ cup water

4 fresh ears corn, shucked and halved

1 teaspoon salt

3 tablespoons unsalted butter, cut into 4 pats

1 Add milk, water, and corn to the Instant Pot®. Sprinkle with salt and place butter pats on corn. Lock lid.

2 Press the Manual or Pressure Cook button and adjust time to 2 minutes. When timer beeps, quick-release pressure until float valve drops. Unlock lid. Toss corn twice in pot liquids.

3 Transfer corn to a platter. Serve warm.

PER SERVING:

CALORIES: 60 | FAT: 2g | PROTEIN: 2g | SODIUM: 132mg | FIBER: 1g | CARBOHYDRATES: 11g | NET CARBS: 10g | SUGAR: 3g

Glazed Cooked Carrots

Carrots already have a slightly sweet note to their nature, and with the addition of a little maple syrup and seasonings, that sweetness is only amplified. With your Instant Pot®, this delicious side dish cooks in only 5 minutes, so now you have no excuse not to eat your carrots!

Pantry Staples: salt
Hands-On Time: 10 minutes
Cook Time: 5 minutes

Serves 6

1 pound carrots, peeled and
   sliced into ½" pieces
¼ cup maple syrup
¼ teaspoon salt
3 tablespoons unsalted
   butter, cut into 3 pats
1 cup water

1 In a medium bowl, toss carrots in maple syrup. Season with salt. Add to a glass baking dish. Place butter pats on top of carrots.

2 Add water to the Instant Pot® and insert steam rack. Lower dish onto steam rack. Lock lid.

3 Press the Manual or Pressure Cook button and adjust time to 5 minutes. When timer beeps, let pressure release naturally until float valve drops. Unlock lid.

4 Remove dish from pot and stir carrots. Serve warm.

PER SERVING:

CALORIES: 115 | FAT: 5g | PROTEIN: 1g | SODIUM: 150mg | FIBER: 2g | CARBOHYDRATES: 16g | NET CARBS: 14g | SUGAR: 11g

7

Chicken Main Dishes

Not only is chicken relatively inexpensive, but it is also one of the most consumed proteins in the United States. There are a million recipes and a handful of go-to meals that you can cook for your family. But if you're sick of eating dried-out chicken breast and overcooked thighs, the Instant Pot® is your new best friend. The steam and pressure used to cook items in the pot are guaranteed to leave the chicken dishes in this chapter juicy and delicious! Whether you're craving Buttermilk Cornish Game Hens or Cheesy Chicken Chile Verde, or your family is calling for BBQ Shredded Chicken Sandwiches or Creamy Pesto Chicken, you'll find a new favorite recipe here!

Also, if you're planning on getting home late, the Instant Pot® allows you to start a meal in the morning and set it to automatically switch to the Keep Warm function for up to 10 hours, which means dinner will be ready and waiting when you walk in the door. So get cooking!

Whole "Rotisserie" Chicken

Sometimes, that rotisserie chicken is an easy grab item at the grocery store. But what if you could pay less and cook it on your own? Prep your chicken in minutes and go take your well-deserved bubble bath. Come back and your chicken is done. Don't forget to save the carcass for some nutritional homemade broth that can be turned into a delicious soup within the next few days!

Pantry Staples: none
Hands-On Time: 10 minutes
Cook Time: 25 minutes

Serves 4

1 (5-pound) whole chicken
1 tablespoon rotisserie chicken seasoning mix
1 small apple of your choice, quartered and cored
1 medium lemon, quartered
2 cups water

ROTISSERIE CHICKEN SEASONING MIX

You can buy this seasoning mix already prepared, or you can make it by combining these common spices:
1 tablespoon smoked paprika,
1 tablespoon dried thyme,
2 teaspoons garlic powder,
1 tablespoon onion powder,
1 teaspoon cayenne pepper,
1 tablespoon salt, and
1 teaspoon ground black pepper.

1 Pat chicken dry, inside and out, with paper towels. Sprinkle chicken with chicken seasoning mix. Place apple and lemon pieces in cavity of chicken.

2 Add water to the Instant Pot® and insert steam rack. Place chicken on steam rack. Lock lid.

3 Press the Manual or Pressure Cook button and adjust time to 25 minutes. When timer beeps, let pressure release naturally until float valve drops. Unlock lid. Check chicken using a meat thermometer to ensure internal temperature is at least 165°F.

4 Remove chicken from pot. Discard apple and lemon pieces. Serve warm.

PER SERVING:

CALORIES: 634 | FAT: 37g | PROTEIN: 60g | SODIUM: 492mg | FIBER: 0g | CARBOHYDRATES: 0g | NET CARBS: 0g | SUGAR: 0g

Buttermilk Cornish Game Hens

Marinating chicken in buttermilk helps tenderize the meat in addition to adding a little tangy zip to the dish. Eight hours is usually the standard time of a buttermilk brine.

Pantry Staples: Italian seasoning, salt, ground black pepper, olive oil
Hands-On Time: 10 minutes
Cook Time: 15 minutes

Serves 2

- 2 (1½-pound) Cornish game hens
- 2 cups buttermilk
- 2 tablespoons Italian seasoning
- 2 teaspoons chili powder
- 1 teaspoon salt
- ½ teaspoon ground black pepper
- 1 medium orange, quartered
- 1½ cups water
- 1 tablespoon olive oil

1 Pat down Cornish game hens with a paper towel. Set aside.

2 In a large bowl, whisk together buttermilk, Italian seasoning, chili powder, salt, and pepper. Place hens in mixture. Refrigerate covered overnight.

3 Place orange quarters in cavities of hens.

4 Add water to the Instant Pot®. Insert steamer basket and place hens in basket. Lock lid.

5 Press the Meat button and adjust time to 10 minutes. When timer beeps, let pressure release naturally for 5 minutes. Quick-release any additional pressure until float valve drops. Unlock lid. Check hens using a meat thermometer to ensure internal temperature is at least 165°F.

6 Transfer hens to a parchment paper–lined baking sheet and brush hens with oil. Remove and discard orange quarters from cavities of hens. Broil 5 minutes.

7 Transfer hens to a serving dish. Serve warm.

PER SERVING:

CALORIES: 734 | FAT: 50g | PROTEIN: 58g | SODIUM: 313mg | FIBER: 0g | CARBOHYDRATES: 1g | NET CARBS: 1g | SUGAR: 1g

Insalata Caprese Chicken Bowls

The addition of chicken to this classic salad originating on the island of Capri adds yet another delicious element to this already fresh salad. Representing the colors of the Italian flag—green (fresh basil), white (mozzarella), and red (tomatoes)—this dish is best enjoyed with a fine glass of Italian vino!

Pantry Staples: salt, ground black pepper, olive oil
Hands-On Time: 10 minutes
Cook Time: 5 minutes

Serves 4

- 1½ pounds boneless, skinless chicken breasts, cut into 1" cubes
- 1 (28-ounce) can diced tomatoes, including juice
- ½ teaspoon salt
- ½ teaspoon ground black pepper
- 1 (8-ounce) container fresh ciliegine mozzarella, drained and halved
- 1 tablespoon olive oil
- 2 tablespoons balsamic vinegar
- ½ cup julienned fresh basil leaves

WHAT ARE *CILIEGINE*?
Ciliegine, which translates to "cherry-sized," are bite-sized fresh mozzarella balls. They are made with 100 percent whole cow's milk and, traditionally, buffalo milk. The liquid that they are stored in is actually whey and keeps the cheese moist and creamy.

1 In the Instant Pot®, add chicken and tomatoes. Lock lid.

2 Press the Manual or Pressure Cook button and adjust time to 5 minutes. When timer beeps, let pressure release naturally for 10 minutes. Quick-release any additional pressure until float valve drops. Unlock lid. Check chicken using a meat thermometer to ensure internal temperature is at least 165°F.

3 Using a slotted spoon, transfer chicken and tomatoes to four bowls. Season with salt and pepper. Add mozzarella halves. Drizzle with oil and balsamic vinegar. Garnish with basil. Serve immediately.

PER SERVING:

CALORIES: 433 | FAT: 17g | PROTEIN: 54g | SODIUM: 886mg | FIBER: 3g | CARBOHYDRATES: 12g | NET CARBS: 9g | SUGAR: 6g

Lemon-Butter Chicken and Fingerling Potatoes

You have one pot cooking with this meal. The exquisite flavor combo of lemon and butter makes anything taste better.

Pantry Staples: salt, ground black pepper, chicken broth
Hands-On Time: 5 minutes
Cook Time: 10 minutes

Serves 8

- 3 pounds boneless and skinless chicken thighs
- 1 teaspoon salt
- ½ teaspoon ground black pepper
- 2 pounds fingerling potatoes, halved
- 1 large sweet onion, peeled and large-chopped
- 1 cup chicken broth
- 1 medium lemon, halved, divided
- 4 tablespoons unsalted butter, cut into 8 pats, divided

1 Season chicken with salt and pepper.

2 Layer potatoes and onion in the Instant Pot®. Pour in broth. Place chicken on top. Squeeze half of lemon over chicken. Add 4 butter pats. Lock lid.

3 Press the Manual or Pressure Cook button and adjust time to 10 minutes. When timer beeps, let pressure release naturally for 10 minutes. Quick-release any additional pressure until float valve drops. Unlock lid. Check chicken using a meat thermometer to make sure internal temperature is at least 165°F.

4 Using a slotted spoon, remove chicken, potatoes, and onions and transfer to a platter. Squeeze remaining half of lemon over platter. Top with remaining 4 butter pats. Serve warm.

PER SERVING:

CALORIES: 265 | **FAT:** 11g | **PROTEIN:** 19g | **SODIUM:** 370mg | **FIBER:** 3g | **CARBOHYDRATES:** 20g | **NET CARBS:** 17g | **SUGAR:** 2g

Cheesy Chicken Chile Verde

Creamy, ooey-gooey cheese with the slight zing of the green chiles makes this chicken irresistible. Served over rice, this complete meal will be on your table in under 30 minutes; allow your Instant Pot® to do all of the work!

Pantry Staples: salt, ground black pepper
Hands-On Time: 10 minutes
Cook Time: 13 minutes

Serves 4

1 pound boneless, skinless chicken breasts, cut in 1" cubes
1 teaspoon salt
½ teaspoon ground black pepper
2 cups water
2 (4-ounce) cans diced green chiles
½ cup shredded Colby jack cheese
4 cups cooked rice

1 Season chicken with salt and pepper.

2 Preheat oven to broiler at 500°F.

3 Add water to the Instant Pot® and insert steam rack. Add chicken and green chiles to baking dish and place on steam rack. Lock lid.

4 Press the Manual or Pressure Cook button and adjust time to 10 minutes. When timer beeps, let pressure release naturally for 10 minutes. Quick-release any additional pressure until float valve drops. Unlock lid. Check chicken using a meat thermometer to ensure internal temperature is at least 165°F.

5 Line a baking sheet with parchment paper. Transfer chicken to prepared baking sheet. Sprinkle cheese evenly over chicken.

6 Place sheet under a broiler 3 minutes.

7 Serve warm over rice.

PER SERVING:

CALORIES: 436 | FAT: 7g | PROTEIN: 33g | SODIUM: 897mg | FIBER: 3g | CARBOHYDRATES: 58g | NET CARBS: 55g | SUGAR: 2g

Black Bean and Corn Salsa Chicken Breasts

Dinner couldn't be easier than this dish. Dump everything into your Instant Pot®, and by the time you get your frozen margaritas made, dinner will just about be ready!

Pantry Staples: chicken broth
Hands-On Time: 5 minutes
Cook Time: 15 minutes

Serves 4

2 pounds boneless, skinless chicken breasts
1 (16-ounce) jar black bean and corn salsa
½ cup chicken broth

1 Place all ingredients in the Instant Pot®. Lock lid.

2 Press the Manual or Pressure Cook button and adjust time to 15 minutes. When timer beeps, let pressure release naturally for 10 minutes. Quick-release any additional pressure until float valve drops. Unlock lid. Check chicken using a meat thermometer to ensure internal temperature is at least 165°F.

3 Transfer chicken and salsa to a serving dish. Serve warm.

PER SERVING:

CALORIES: 321 | FAT: 5g | PROTEIN: 54g | SODIUM: 961mg | FIBER: 1g | CARBOHYDRATES: 11g | NET CARBS: 10g | SUGAR: 4g

BBQ Shredded Chicken Sandwiches

Tired of the plain chicken breast? Change it up and shred it any variety of barbecue sauce. Pick your favorite bun and enjoy!

Pantry Staples: chicken broth
Hands-On Time: 10 minutes
Cook Time: 15 minutes

Serves 6

- 1 cup chicken broth
- 2 pounds boneless, skinless chicken breasts
- 2 cups barbecue sauce
- 1 small sweet onion, peeled and grated
- 6 hamburger buns
- 24 dill pickle slices

1 Add broth, chicken breasts, barbecue sauce, and onion to the Instant Pot®. Lock lid.

2 Press the Manual or Pressure Cook button and adjust time to 15 minutes. When timer beeps, let pressure release naturally for 10 minutes. Quick-release any additional pressure until float valve drops. Unlock lid. Check chicken using a meat thermometer to ensure internal temperature is at least 165°F.

3 Using two forks, pull apart chicken in pot. Using a slotted spoon, transfer chicken to hamburger buns and place 4 pickle slices on each. Serve warm.

PER SERVING:

CALORIES: 471 | **FAT:** 5g | **PROTEIN:** 43g | **SODIUM:** 1,485mg | **FIBER:** 2g | **CARBOHYDRATES:** 62g | **NET CARBS:** 60g | **SUGAR:** 35g

Chicken and Gnocchi Alfredo with Vegetables

This is a great dish for already prepped and cooked chicken that you need to use. The gnocchi used in this recipe is found in the pasta aisle, not the frozen section.

Pantry Staples: chicken broth
Hands-On Time: 10 minutes
Cook Time: 3 minutes

Serves 6

1 (16-ounce) package gnocchi
1 (16-ounce) jar Alfredo sauce
½ cup chicken broth
1 cup chopped cooked chicken
1 (6.5-ounce) can mushroom stems and pieces, drained
1 (8.5-ounce) can sweet peas and carrots, drained

1 In the Instant Pot®, add gnocchi and sauce. Pour broth into empty sauce jar, close lid of jar, and shake. Pour mixture into pot. Stir in remaining ingredients. Lock lid.

2 Press the Manual or Pressure Cook button and adjust time to 3 minutes. When timer beeps, let pressure release naturally for 5 minutes. Quick-release any additional pressure until float valve drops. Unlock lid.

3 Transfer to bowls. Serve warm.

PER SERVING:

CALORIES: 316 | FAT: 8g | PROTEIN: 14g | SODIUM: 948mg | FIBER: 3g | CARBOHYDRATES: 33g | NET CARBS: 30g | SUGAR: 0g

Chicken Salad

Crunchy, creamy, sweet, and savory...this Chicken Salad hits all of the notes. Serve this salad on buns, in lettuce wraps for lighter days, or on crackers for your guests.

Pantry Staples: chicken broth, salt, ground black pepper
Hands-On Time: 15 minutes
Cook Time: 15 minutes

Serves 6

1 cup chicken broth
2 pounds boneless, skinless chicken breasts
2 medium stalks celery, diced
1 cup chopped pecans
1½ cups mayonnaise
1 tablespoon Dijon mustard
½ teaspoon salt
¼ teaspoon ground black pepper

1 Add broth and chicken to the Instant Pot®. Lock lid.

2 Press the Manual or Pressure Cook button and adjust time to 15 minutes. When timer beeps, let pressure release naturally for 10 minutes. Quick-release any additional pressure until float valve drops. Unlock lid. Check chicken using a meat thermometer to ensure the internal temperature is at least 165°F.

3 Using two forks, pull apart chicken in pot.

4 Using a slotted spoon, transfer chicken to a large bowl. Stir in remaining ingredients. Refrigerate until chilled. Serve.

PER SERVING:

CALORIES: 689 | FAT: 57g | PROTEIN: 40g | SODIUM: 686mg | FIBER: 2g | CARBOHYDRATES: 4g | NET CARBS: 2g | SUGAR: 1g

Creamy Pesto Chicken

What's better than pesto? Creamy pesto! Never get tired of this simple dish by purchasing different pesto flavors available on shelves at the grocery store, or get creative with different herbs and nuts and make your own.

Pantry Staples: all-purpose flour, salt, ground black pepper
Hands-On Time: 5 minutes
Cook Time: 10 minutes

Serves 6

½ cup pesto
¾ cup heavy cream
1 tablespoon all-purpose flour
2 tablespoons grated Parmesan cheese
2 cloves garlic, peeled and minced
¼ teaspoon salt
½ teaspoon ground black pepper
3 pounds boneless and skinless chicken thighs
1 cup water

1 In a medium bowl, whisk together pesto, cream, flour, cheese, garlic, salt, and pepper.

2 Add chicken to a 7-cup glass baking dish. Pour pesto mixture over chicken.

3 Add water to the Instant Pot® and insert steam rack. Place glass baking dish on steam rack. Lock lid.

4 Press the Manual or Pressure Cook button and adjust time to 10 minutes. When timer beeps, let pressure release naturally for 10 minutes. Quick-release any additional pressure until float valve drops. Unlock lid. Check chicken using a meat thermometer to ensure internal temperature is at least 165°F.

5 Carefully remove dish from pot. Serve warm.

PER SERVING:

CALORIES: 510 | FAT: 31g | PROTEIN: 42g | SODIUM: 457mg | FIBER: 3g | CARBOHYDRATES: 10g | NET CARBS: 7g | SUGAR: 1g

PESTO 101

Homemade pesto is easy to make and has an amazing shelf life. Pulse the following ingredients in a small food processor: 1 cup fresh basil leaves, 1 cup fresh parsley leaves, ½ cup olive oil, ⅓ cup pine nuts, ½ cup freshly grated Parmesan cheese, 3–5 cloves garlic, ½ teaspoon salt, and ¼ teaspoon ground black pepper.

Island Chicken Legs

Planning a staycation? Don't forget about your menu. You'll imagine being at a luau by the ocean while eating these salty-sweet chicken legs.

Pantry Staples: granulated sugar, garlic salt
Hands-On Time: 10 minutes
Cook Time: 21 minutes

Serves 5

1 (8-ounce) can pineapple, including juice
2 tablespoons tomato paste
¼ cup granulated sugar
2 tablespoons soy sauce
2 teaspoons grated fresh ginger
1 teaspoon garlic salt
3 pounds (about 10) chicken legs/drumsticks
1 cup water

1 In a blender, combine pineapple, tomato paste, sugar, soy sauce, ginger, and garlic salt. Divide sauce in half. Add chicken legs to half of mixture and refrigerate 30 minutes.

2 Preheat oven to broiler at 500°F.

3 Add water to the Instant Pot® and insert steam rack. Arrange chicken standing up, meaty side down, on steam rack. Lock lid.

4 Press the Poultry button and cook for the default time of 15 minutes. When timer beeps, let pressure release naturally for 5 minutes. Quick-release any additional pressure until float valve drops. Unlock lid. Check chicken using a meat thermometer to ensure internal temperature is at least 165°F.

5 Place chicken legs on a parchment paper–lined baking sheet and broil 3 minutes on each side to crisp chicken. Toss chicken in remaining sauce mixture.

6 Transfer chicken to a platte. Serve warm.

PER SERVING:

CALORIES: 624 | FAT: 29g | PROTEIN: 61g | SODIUM: 976mg | FIBER: 1g | CARBOHYDRATES: 19g | NET CARBS: 18g | SUGAR: 17g

Moroccan-Inspired Chicken Thighs

Don't overlook that beautiful juice in the olive jar, as it proves to make a very tasty brine. Add this to the spicy seasonings to create a flavor explosion for these already juicy chicken thighs.

Pantry Staples: salt, ground black pepper
Hands-On Time: 10 minutes
Cook Time: 7 minutes

Serves 6

2 teaspoons smoked paprika
1 teaspoon cumin
½ teaspoon ground ginger
1 teaspoon salt
½ teaspoon ground black pepper
3 pounds boneless, skinless chicken thighs
1 cup water
½ cup sliced Manzanilla green olives plus ¼ cup juice from jar

ADD IT IN!

There are at least two ways to step up this recipe. You can add ½ teaspoon ground cinnamon to the spice mix. Or you can add 2–3 minced garlic cloves to the olive juice. Do both or do neither. This dish is loaded with flavor!

1 In a small bowl, combine paprika, cumin, ginger, salt, and pepper.

2 Pat chicken dry with a paper towel. Season with spice mixture.

3 Add water to the Instant Pot® and insert steam rack. Add olive juice to a 7-cup glass baking dish. Arrange chicken in dish. Scatter olives evenly over chicken. Lock lid.

4 Press the Manual or Pressure Cook button and adjust time to 7 minutes. When timer beeps, quick-release pressure until float valve drops. Unlock lid. Check chicken using a meat thermometer to ensure internal temperature is at least 165°F.

5 Remove dish from pot. Serve warm.

PER SERVING:

CALORIES: 358 | FAT: 17g | PROTEIN: 42g | SODIUM: 831mg | FIBER: 1g | CARBOHYDRATES: 1g | NET CARBS: 0g | SUGAR: 0g

Mozzarella Chicken Meatballs

You will lighten your meatball load by using ground chicken instead of pork or beef, but don't worry. The addition of the melty mozzarella and savory marinara will work in conjunction to elevate the flavor of this lighter dish.

Pantry Staples: Italian seasoning, ground black pepper, olive oil
Hands-On Time: 15 minutes
Cook Time: 16 minutes

Serves 4

1 pound ground chicken
1 large egg, lightly beaten
¼ cup panko bread crumbs
1 tablespoon Italian seasoning
½ teaspoon ground black pepper
¾ cup shredded mozzarella cheese, divided
2 tablespoons olive oil, divided
1 (24-ounce) jar marinara sauce

1 In a medium bowl, combine chicken, egg, bread crumbs, Italian seasoning, pepper, and ¼ cup cheese. Form into sixteen golf ball–sized meatballs. Set aside.

2 Press the Sauté button on the Instant Pot® and heat 1 tablespoon oil. Place half the meatballs around the edges of the pot. Sear all sides of meatballs for a total of 4 minutes. Remove first batch and set aside a paper towel–lined plate. Add remaining oil and meatballs and sear 4 minutes. Press the Cancel button. Remove meatballs.

3 Discard extra juice and oil from pot.

4 Place meatballs evenly on bottom of pot. Add marinara sauce. Lock lid.

5 Press the Manual or Pressure Cook button and adjust time to 3 minutes. When timer beeps, quick-release pressure until float valve drops. Unlock lid. Check chicken using a meat thermometer to ensure internal temperature is at least 165°F.

6 Add remaining cheese in an even layer over meatballs. Let simmer lidded 5 minutes, allowing cheese to melt.

7 Transfer meatballs and sauce to bowls. Serve warm.

PER SERVING:

CALORIES: 411 | FAT: 22g | PROTEIN: 30g | SODIUM: 956mg | FIBER: 3g | CARBOHYDRATES: 19g | NET CARBS: 16g | SUGAR: 10g

Nashville Hot Chicken Patties

You'll feel like you are at Nashville's popular Hattie B's when you take a bite of these patties. Add less or more heat to your liking. They're best served on some Texas toast with sweet pickle slices and a dollop of mayonnaise-based coleslaw! I recommend using Tabasco brand hot sauce for this recipe.

Pantry Staples: hot sauce, salt, ground black pepper
Hands-On Time: 10 minutes
Cook Time: 10 minutes

Serves 4

1 pound ground chicken
½ medium sweet onion, peeled and grated
1 tablespoon hot sauce
1 teaspoon chili powder
1 teaspoon cayenne pepper
1 teaspoon packed light brown sugar
1 teaspoon salt
½ teaspoon ground black pepper
1 cup water

1 In a small bowl, combine chicken, onion, hot sauce, chili powder, cayenne pepper, brown sugar, salt, and black pepper. Form into four patties. Wrap each one in aluminum foil.

2 Add water to the Instant Pot® and insert steam rack. Arrange patties on steam rack. Lock lid.

3 Press the Manual or Pressure Cook button and adjust time to 10 minutes. When timer beeps, quick-release pressure until float valve drops. Unlock lid. Check chicken using a meat thermometer to ensure internal temperature is at least 165°F.

4 Remove patties from pot. Serve warm.

PER SERVING:

CALORIES: 175 | **FAT:** 9g | **PROTEIN:** 20g | **SODIUM:** 784mg | **FIBER:** 1g | **CARBOHYDRATES:** 3g | **NET CARBS:** 2g | **SUGAR:** 2g

Honey-Lime Chicken Legs

The acid from the limes and smokiness from the ground cumin balance out the golden sweetness of the honey on these chicken legs. These are addictive. You've been warned.

Pantry Staples: garlic salt
Hands-On Time: 5 minutes
Cook Time: 21 minutes

Serves 5

Juice and zest from 2 medium limes, divided
4 tablespoons honey
1 tablespoon ground cumin
3 pounds (about 10) chicken legs/drumsticks
1 teaspoon garlic salt
1 cup water

1 In a medium bowl, combine lime juice, all but 2 teaspoons lime zest, honey, and cumin. Set aside.

2 Season chicken with garlic salt.

3 Add water to the Instant Pot® and insert steam rack. Arrange chicken standing up, meaty side down, on steam rack. Lock lid.

4 Press the Poultry button and cook for the default time of 15 minutes. When timer beeps, let pressure release naturally for 5 minutes. Quick-release any additional pressure until float valve drops. Unlock lid. Check chicken using a meat thermometer to ensure internal temperature is at least 165°F.

5 Toss chicken in honey-lime mixture. Place chicken legs on a baking sheet and broil 3 minutes on each side to crisp chicken skin.

6 Transfer chicken to a platter and garnish with remaining lime zest. Serve warm.

PER SERVING:

CALORIES: 609 | FAT: 29g | PROTEIN: 61g | SODIUM: 578mg | FIBER: 1g | CARBOHYDRATES: 15g | NET CARBS: 14g | SUGAR: 14g

Chicken Taco Salad Bowls

What a perfect meal for Taco Tuesday! It's inexpensive and quick, and you can set out an assortment of taco salad toppings for each to individualize their taco bowls. Sour cream, black olives, guacamole, salsa, and diced tomatoes are just a few toppings to display.

Pantry Staples: olive oil, hot sauce
Hands-On Time: 15 minutes
Cook Time: 4 minutes

Serves 4

2 teaspoons olive oil
1 pound ground chicken
1 (1.25-ounce) packet taco seasoning mix
⅛ teaspoon hot sauce
½ cup water
4 cups shredded iceberg lettuce
¼ cup shredded Mexican-blend cheese
1 cup crushed tortilla chips

1 Press the Sauté button on the Instant Pot®. Heat olive oil. Add chicken and brown 3 minutes.

2 Stir in taco seasoning mix, hot sauce, and water. Press the Cancel button. Lock lid.

3 Press the Manual or Pressure Cook button and adjust time to 1 minute. When timer beeps, quick-release pressure until float valve drops. Unlock lid. Stir mixture.

4 Line four bowls with lettuce. Using a slotted spoon, transfer chicken mixture to bowls. Garnish with cheese and tortilla chips. Serve warm.

PER SERVING:

CALORIES: 322 | FAT: 16g | PROTEIN: 24g | SODIUM: 789mg | FIBER: 3g | CARBOHYDRATES: 18g | NET CARBS: 15g | SUGAR: 3g

GROUND CHICKEN DIFFERENCES

You may notice that there are varieties of ground chicken, using both white and dark meat. Although white meat is lower in calories because it is leaner, dark chicken meat is less dry and generally tastier because it has a higher natural fat percentage. Both are fine choices; it's just a matter of personal preference.

Pickleback Wings

Don't you dare throw away that pickle juice! It makes a beautiful brine for chicken and pork. As far as the hot sauce goes, whether it is sriracha, Tabasco, or your favorite local brand, they all work beautifully with this recipe.

Pantry Staples: hot sauce, garlic salt, ground black pepper
Hands-On Time: 10 minutes
Cook Time: 16 minutes

Serves 6

2 pounds chicken wings
1 cup dill pickle juice
1 tablespoon packed dark brown sugar
1 tablespoon hot sauce
¼ teaspoon garlic salt
¼ teaspoon ground black pepper
½ cup bourbon whiskey
1 cup dill pickle slices

1 In a medium bowl, combine chicken wings and pickle juice. Refrigerate 1 hour.

2 In a large bowl, combine brown sugar, hot sauce, garlic salt, and pepper. Set aside.

3 If you buy chicken wings that are connected, cut them at the joint to separate. Set aside.

4 Add chicken wings, pickle juice brine, and bourbon whiskey to the Instant Pot®. Lock lid.

5 Press the Manual or Pressure Cook button and adjust time to 10 minutes. When timer beeps, let pressure release naturally for 5 minutes. Quick-release any additional pressure until float valve drops. Unlock lid.

6 Add chicken wings to spice mixture and toss. Line a baking sheet with parchment paper. Transfer wings to prepared baking sheet. Broil 3 minutes. Flip wings and broil for an additional 3 minutes.

7 Transfer wings to a plate and garnish with pickle slices. Serve warm.

PER SERVING:

CALORIES: 349 | FAT: 21g | PROTEIN: 31g | SODIUM: 633mg | FIBER: 0g | CARBOHYDRATES: 4g | NET CARBS: 4g | SUGAR: 3g

8

Beef and Pork Main Dishes

If you use your Instant Pot® only for meats, you would still get your money's worth—and more. The steam and pressure can take a tough and inexpensive piece of meat and make it taste like butter in your mouth. The steam keeps everything moist, and the pressure helps break down some of the fat and the sinewy parts. And the best part? Within 30 minutes, the trapped steam helps create meat that tastes like it has been braised for hours, depending on the weight of the meat.

With recipes ranging from Italian Beef Sandwiches and Pizza Dogs to BBQ Pork Ribs and Classic Meatloaf, this chapter will help get you started on some traditional Instant Pot® recipes as well as give you a starting point to create some of your own.

Pot Roast, Potatoes, and Gravy

This dish will remind you of your grandma's famous dish, only instead of taking all day to cook, it will be ready in a fraction of the time in your Instant Pot®.

Pantry Staples: garlic salt, ground black pepper, olive oil, beef broth, Italian seasoning
Hands-On Time: 10 minutes
Cook Time: 50 minutes

Serves 8

- 1 (3-pound) chuck roast, fat trimmed
- 1 teaspoon garlic salt
- 1 teaspoon ground black pepper
- 1 tablespoon olive oil
- 3 cups beef broth
- 1 tablespoon tomato paste
- 2 teaspoons Worcestershire sauce
- 1 tablespoon Italian seasoning
- 2 pounds baby gold potatoes
- 2 tablespoons cornstarch

1 Season roast with garlic salt and pepper.

2 Press the Sauté button on the Instant Pot® and heat oil. Sear meat on all sides approximately 4–5 minutes. Add broth, scraping brown bits from bottom and sides of pot. Add tomato paste, Worcestershire sauce, Italian seasoning, and potatoes. Press the Cancel button. Lock lid.

3 Press the Manual or Pressure Cook button and adjust time to 45 minutes. When timer beeps, let pressure release naturally for 5 minutes. Quick-release any additional pressure until float valve drops. Unlock lid.

4 Using a slotted spoon transfer meat and potatoes to a platter.

5 Spoon ½ cup liquid from pot into a small bowl and whisk in cornstarch to create a slurry. Whisk slurry back into pot with remaining liquid. Allow to rest and thicken while your roast rests 7 minutes.

6 Slice roast and serve with potatoes and gravy. Serve warm.

PER SERVING:

CALORIES: 345 | **FAT:** 8g | **PROTEIN:** 40g | **SODIUM:** 398mg | **FIBER:** 3g | **CARBOHYDRATES:** 22g | **NET CARBS:** 19g | **SUGAR:** 1g

Seasoned Flank Steak

Flank steak is the most underutilized steak. It is inexpensive and often tossed to the side. But guess what? Give it a good marinade and slice it correctly (against the grain), and it can compete with the best of cuts out there.

Pantry Staples: salt, olive oil, beef broth
Hands-On Time: 10 minutes
Cook Time: 20 minutes

Serves 8

- ⅓ cup fresh-squeezed orange juice
- 2 tablespoons honey
- 2 teaspoons ground cumin
- 1 teaspoon salt
- 1 tablespoon sriracha
- 3 tablespoons olive oil, divided
- 2 pounds flank steak
- 1½ cups beef broth

1 In a small bowl, combine orange juice, honey, cumin, salt, sriracha, and 2 tablespoons oil. Place mixture and flank steak in a large sealable plastic bag. Seal, then massage mixture into meat through the bag. Refrigerate 1 hour.

2 Press the Sauté button on the Instant Pot® and heat remaining 1 tablespoon oil. Sear meat on all sides, approximately 4–5 minutes. Add broth to deglaze pot, scraping any bits from the bottom and sides of pot. Press the Cancel button. Lock lid.

3 Press the Manual or Pressure Cook button and adjust time to 15 minutes. When timer beeps, let pressure release naturally for 10 minutes. Quick-release any additional pressure until float valve drops. Unlock lid.

4 Transfer meat to a serving platter. Thinly slice and serve.

PER SERVING:

CALORIES: 285 | FAT: 17g | PROTEIN: 25g | SODIUM: 245mg | FIBER: 0g | CARBOHYDRATES: 3g | NET CARBS: 3g | SUGAR: 3g

Italian Beef Sandwiches

You don't have to travel to Chicago to enjoy one of the city's original recipes with thin slices of beef, slivered peppers, and chopped pickled vegetables known as *giardiniera*. The bread of this sandwich is usually "wet," meaning that it has been dipped in au jus, or "gravy," as the locals call it, which is the liquid that the meat and peppers were cooked in.

Pantry Staples: olive oil, Italian seasoning, hot sauce, garlic salt, ground black pepper, beef broth
Hands-On Time: 15 minutes
Cook Time: 65 minutes

Serves 8

¼ cup olive oil
1 tablespoon Italian seasoning
2 teaspoons hot sauce
1 teaspoon garlic salt
½ teaspoon ground black pepper
3 medium bell peppers, variety of colors, seeded and sliced
1 large yellow onion, peeled and sliced
1 (3-pound) boneless chuck roast, quartered
4 cups beef broth
8 hoagie rolls
1 cup chopped jarred *giardiniera*, drained

1 In a large bowl, combine oil, Italian seasoning, hot sauce, garlic salt, and black pepper. Add bell peppers, onion, and roast and toss. Refrigerate covered at least 30 minutes or up to overnight.

2 Press the Sauté button on the Instant Pot® and add meat, vegetables, and marinade. Sear meat 5 minutes, making sure to brown each side. Add broth. Press the Cancel button. Lock lid.

3 Press the Manual or Pressure Cook button and adjust time to 60 minutes. When timer beeps, let pressure release naturally for 5 minutes. Quick-release any additional pressure until float valve drops. Unlock lid. Strain all but ¼ cup liquid from pot. Set strained liquid aside for dipping.

4 Transfer meat to a cutting board. Let meat rest 5 minutes, then thinly slice roast and add back to pot with vegetables and remaining pot liquid to moisten meat.

5 Using a slotted spoon, transfer meat to rolls, garnish with *giardiniera*, and serve with dipping liquid.

PER SERVING:

CALORIES: 541 | FAT: 19g | PROTEIN: 51g | SODIUM: 820mg | FIBER: 3g | CARBOHYDRATES: 40g | NET CARBS: 37g | SUGAR: 5g

Beef Shawarma Bowls

With origins in Middle Eastern cuisine, shawarma is traditionally cooked on a rotisserie and sliced as it cooks, ensuring that each bite of meat is both crisp and juicy. This dish is delicious served as a salad over arugula or stuffed into a fresh pita. Unlike its similar Greek counterpart, the gyro, shawarma is never served with tzatziki sauce.

Pantry Staples: olive oil
Hands-On Time: 10 minutes
Cook Time: 3 minutes

Serves 4

- 1 (1-pound) boneless sirloin, trimmed and sliced into 3" strips
- 2 tablespoons shawarma seasoning mix
- 1 tablespoon olive oil
- 1 cup water
- 3 medium Roma tomatoes, diced
- 1 small red onion, peeled and sliced
- 1 cup hummus

SHAWARMA SEASONING

You can purchase premixed shawarma seasoning mix or make your own. Combine: ¼ cup ground black pepper, 2 tablespoons ground allspice, 2 tablespoons garlic powder, 2 tablespoons ground cloves, 2 tablespoons ground cinnamon, 1 tablespoon ground nutmeg, 1 tablespoon ground cardamom, 1 tablespoon chili powder, 1 tablespoon dried oregano, and 2 teaspoons salt.

1 In a medium bowl, combine sirloin and shawarma seasoning mix. Refrigerate covered 30 minutes.

2 Press the Sauté button on the Instant Pot® and heat oil. Place sirloin in pot and stir-fry 2 minutes, then transfer to steamer basket. Press the Cancel button.

3 Add water to the Instant Pot® and insert basket. Lock lid.

4 Press the Manual or Pressure Cook button and adjust time to 1 minute. When timer beeps, quick-release pressure until float valve drops. Unlock lid.

5 Transfer beef to bowls and garnish with tomatoes, onion, and hummus. Serve warm.

PER SERVING:

CALORIES: 341 | **FAT:** 14g | **PROTEIN:** 33g | **SODIUM:** 412mg | **FIBER:** 5g | **CARBOHYDRATES:** 18g | **NET CARBS:** 13g | **SUGAR:** 2g

Easy Ground Bulgogi

Traditionally made with thin slices of beef, this Korean barbecue has been simplified for time and cost—all the flavor, none of the hassle. This dish is excellent served over rice or even in lettuce wraps. Either sriracha or gochujang are the recommended hot sauces for this recipe.

Pantry Staples: olive oil, granulated sugar, hot sauce
Hands-On Time: 10 minutes
Cook Time: 5 minutes

Serves 4

1 tablespoon olive oil
1 pound 80/20 ground beef
3 medium green onions, sliced (whites and greens separated)
3 cloves garlic, peeled and minced
¼ cup soy sauce
¼ cup granulated sugar
2 teaspoons hot sauce
1 teaspoon minced ginger

1 Press the Sauté button on the Instant Pot® and heat oil. Add ground beef and onion whites. Stir-fry 3–4 minutes until onions are tender and beef is almost all brown. Add garlic and heat 1 additional minute.

2 Stir in soy sauce, sugar, hot sauce, and ginger. Press the Cancel button. Lock lid.

3 Press the Manual or Pressure Cook button and adjust time to 0 minutes. When timer beeps, quick-release pressure until float valve drops. Unlock lid.

4 Transfer pot ingredients to bowls. Garnish with onion greens. Serve warm.

PER SERVING:

CALORIES: 351 | FAT: 19g | PROTEIN: 21g | SODIUM: 1,412mg | FIBER: 0g | CARBOHYDRATES: 15g | NET CARBS: 15g | SUGAR: 13g

Melt-in-Your-Mouth Meatballs

As Lemony Snicket once wisely proclaimed, "Miracles are like meatballs, because nobody can exactly agree on what they are made of, where they come from, or how often they should appear." But one thing we can all agree on is that nothing beats a great meatball!

Pantry Staples: Italian seasoning, garlic salt, ground black pepper, olive oil
Hands-On Time: 15 minutes
Cook Time: 16 minutes

Serves 4

1 pound 80/20 ground beef
¼ cup grated Parmesan cheese
1 large egg, lightly beaten
1 tablespoon Italian seasoning
1 cup panko bread crumbs
½ teaspoon garlic salt
½ teaspoon ground black pepper
2 tablespoons olive oil
1 cup marinara sauce
2 cups water

1   In a medium bowl, combine beef, cheese, egg, Italian seasoning, bread crumbs, garlic salt, and pepper. If stiff, add 1–2 tablespoons water. Form mixture into eight meatballs. Set aside.

2   Press the Sauté button on the Instant Pot® and heat oil. Place meatballs around the edge of pot. Sear all sides of meatballs, about 4 minutes total. Press the Cancel button.

3   Transfer seared meatballs to a 7-cup glass baking dish. Top with marinara sauce. Discard extra juice and oil from pot.

4   Add water to the Instant Pot® and insert steam rack. Place glass baking dish on top of steam rack. Lock lid.

5   Press the Manual or Pressure Cook button and adjust time to 12 minutes. When timer beeps, let pressure release naturally for 10 minutes. Quick-release any additional pressure until float valve drops. Unlock lid.

6   Transfer meatballs to plates. Serve warm.

PER SERVING:

CALORIES: 428 | FAT: 20g | PROTEIN: 28g | SODIUM: 776mg | FIBER: 1g | CARBOHYDRATES: 26g | NET CARBS: 25g | SUGAR: 5g

Italian Sloppy Joes

This classic childhood favorite is excellent served alone, but it's also delicious on a bun, mixed with rice, or served over pasta. Or for a late night splurge, spoon some over french fries and then melt some cheese over it!

Pantry Staples: olive oil, hot sauce, granulated sugar, salt, ground black pepper, Italian seasoning
Hands-On Time: 10 minutes
Cook Time: 4 minutes

Serves 8

1 tablespoon olive oil
2 pounds 80/20 ground beef
1 medium yellow onion, peeled and diced
2 medium bell peppers (color of choice), seeded and diced
3 cups marinara sauce
2 tablespoons tomato paste
⅛ teaspoon hot sauce
1 teaspoon granulated sugar
1 teaspoon salt
1 teaspoon ground black pepper
2 teaspoons Italian seasoning

1 Press the Sauté button on the Instant Pot® and heat oil. Add beef, onion, and bell peppers. Stir-fry 4 minutes until onions are tender and beef is mostly browned.

2 Add remaining ingredients to pot. Press the Cancel button. Lock lid.

3 Press the Manual or Pressure Cook button and adjust time to 0 minutes. When timer beeps, quick-release pressure until float valve drops. Unlock lid.

4 Transfer mixture to a large bowl. Serve warm.

PER SERVING:

CALORIES: 371 | **FAT:** 22g | **PROTEIN:** 22g | **SODIUM:** 815mg | **FIBER:** 3g | **CARBOHYDRATES:** 12g | **NET CARBS:** 9g | **SUGAR:** 8g

Takeout Beef and Broccoli

When you want Chinese takeout but you don't want the sodium boost, make your own in your Instant Pot®! You can even purchase some takeout containers to serve your creation in for authenticity. And don't forget your chopsticks!

Pantry Staples: olive oil
Hands-On Time: 10 minutes
Cook Time: 4 minutes

Serves 4

- 1 (1-ounce) packet beef and broccoli seasoning mix
- 2 tablespoons soy sauce
- 1¾ cups water, divided
- 1 (1-pound) boneless sirloin, trimmed and sliced into 3″ strips
- 1 tablespoon olive oil
- 1 medium yellow onion, peeled and sliced into half-moons
- 1 medium head broccoli, chopped into florets

1 In a medium bowl, combine seasoning mix, soy sauce, and ¾ cup water. Set aside 2 tablespoons sauce. Add beef to bowl and toss. Refrigerate 30 minutes.

2 Press the Sauté button on the Instant Pot® and heat oil. Place onion and meat in pot and stir-fry 2 minutes. Add broccoli and toss 1 minute. Press the Cancel button. Transfer pot ingredients to a large bowl.

3 Add remaining 1 cup water to the Instant Pot® and insert steamer basket. Add beef and broccoli mixture to basket. Lock lid.

4 Press the Manual or Pressure Cook button and adjust time to 1 minute. When timer beeps, quick-release pressure until float valve drops. Unlock lid.

5 Transfer beef and broccoli to a serving dish and toss with remaining 2 tablespoons sauce. Serve warm.

PER SERVING:

CALORIES: 299 | FAT: 17g | PROTEIN: 25g | SODIUM: 899mg | FIBER: 1g | CARBOHYDRATES: 10g | NET CARBS: 9g | SUGAR: 3g

Pizza Dogs

Pizza rocks! And hot dogs are a close second. What would happen if these two obviously scrumptious quick foods ran into each other? A delicious and easy Instant Pot® taste sensation!

Pantry Staples: none
Hands-On Time: 10 minutes
Cook Time: 3 minutes

Serves 4

2 cups water
8 beef hot dogs
8 hot dog buns
1 cup jarred pizza sauce
1 cup shredded mozzarella
32 mini pepperoni pieces

1   Add water to the Instant Pot®. Add hot dogs. Lock lid.

2   Press the Manual or Pressure Cook button and adjust time to 0 minutes. When timer beeps, quick-release pressure until float valve drops. Unlock lid.

3   Preheat oven to broiler to 500°F. Assemble Pizza Dogs by adding a hot dog to each bun. Add sauce and cheese evenly to each one. Add 4 pepperoni pieces to each. Place assembled dogs on a parchment paper–lined baking sheet. Broil 2–3 minutes until cheese is melted. Serve warm.

PER SERVING:

CALORIES: 740 | FAT: 38g | PROTEIN: 31g | SODIUM: 1,931mg | FIBER: 3g | CARBOHYDRATES: 52g | NET CARBS: 49g | SUGAR: 10g

Pork Cutlets with Gravy

This is just a good ol' recipe that has stood the test of time. Simple ingredients, little prep, excellent results. Mash some potatoes to serve alongside this beautiful gravy and pork!

Pantry Staples: beef broth
Hands-On Time: 10 minutes
Cook Time: 3 minutes

Serves 4

- 4 (4-ounce) pork cutlets
- 1 (.87-ounce) packet brown gravy mix
- 1 (1-ounce) packet ranch seasoning mix
- 1½ cups beef broth
- 1 tablespoon cornstarch

1 Place cutlets in the Instant Pot®. Add gravy mix, ranch mix, and broth. Lock lid.

2 Press the Manual or Pressure Cook button and adjust time to 3 minutes. When timer beeps, let pressure release naturally for 10 minutes. Quick-release any additional pressure until float valve drops. Unlock lid. Transfer cutlets to a platter, leaving liquid in pot.

3 Add cornstarch to a small bowl. Ladle about 2 tablespoons of pot liquid into bowl. Whisk together to create a slurry. Whisk slurry back into pot to thicken. Ladle gravy over cutlets. Serve warm.

PER SERVING:

CALORIES: 160 | **FAT:** 3g | **PROTEIN:** 21g | **SODIUM:** 1,374mg | **FIBER:** 0g | **CARBOHYDRATES:** 10g | **NET CARBS:** 10g | **SUGAR:** 0g

BBQ Pork Ribs

Sometimes simple is needed with a hectic schedule. Choose your sauce, buy a rack of spareribs, and within an hour, you and your family will be eating barbecue ribs. Don't forget that the Instant Pot® has a timer setting, so the ribs can be ready when you step through your door after a long day.

Pantry Staples: none
Hands-On Time: 10 minutes
Cook Time: 30 minutes

Serves 6

1 rack pork spareribs (approximately 3½ pounds), cut into 2-rib sections
1½ cups barbecue sauce, divided
1 cup water

---

1 In a medium bowl, toss ribs with ¾ cup barbecue sauce. Cover bowl and refrigerate at least 30 minutes or up to overnight.

2 Add water to the Instant Pot® and insert steamer basket. Place ribs standing upright in basket with meaty side facing outward toward pot wall. Lock lid.

3 Press the Manual or Pressure Cook button and adjust time to 30 minutes. When timer beeps, let pressure release naturally until float valve drops. Unlock lid.

4 Transfer ribs to a serving dish and serve warm with remaining ¾ cup barbecue sauce for dipping.

PER SERVING:

CALORIES: 532 | FAT: 28g | PROTEIN: 31g | SODIUM: 830mg | FIBER: 1g | CARBOHYDRATES: 29g | NET CARBS: 28g | SUGAR: 24g

Shroomy Meatballs

Double the recipe on this one and cook in two batches to enjoy them for several days in a variety of meals. Packed with flavor with few ingredients, these meatballs can be served over rice, tossed in sauce, or even added to a top-split bun for a meatball sandwich.

Pantry Staples: salt, ground black pepper, olive oil
Hands-On Time: 15 minutes
Cook Time: 16 minutes

Serves 4

- ½ pound ground pork
- ½ pound 80/20 ground beef
- ½ (10.5-ounce) can condensed cream of mushroom soup
- 1 large egg, lightly beaten
- 1 cup panko bread crumbs
- ½ teaspoon salt
- ½ teaspoon ground black pepper
- 2 tablespoons olive oil
- 2 cups water

1 In a medium bowl, combine pork, beef, soup, egg, bread crumbs, salt, and pepper. Form into eight meatballs. Set aside.

2 Press the Sauté button on the Instant Pot® and heat oil. Place meatballs around the edge of pot. Sear all sides of meatballs, about 4 minutes total. Press the Cancel button.

3 Transfer seared meatballs to a 7-cup glass baking dish. Discard extra juice and oil from pot.

4 Add water to the Instant Pot® and insert steam rack. Place glass baking dish on top of steam rack. Lock lid.

5 Press the Manual or Pressure Cook button and adjust time to 12 minutes. When timer beeps, let pressure release naturally for 10 minutes. Quick-release any additional pressure until float valve drops. Unlock lid.

6 Transfer meatballs to plates. Serve warm.

PER SERVING:

CALORIES: 408 | **FAT:** 22g | **PROTEIN:** 26g | **SODIUM:** 689mg | **FIBER:** 0g | **CARBOHYDRATES:** 23g | **NET CARBS:** 23g | **SUGAR:** 1g

Classic Meatloaf

Whether you make this the night before for next-day meatloaf sandwiches, or serve a slice alongside a mound of mashed potatoes, meatloaf has been a welcomed addition to blue plate specials for decades for good reason. It gives you a food hug.

Pantry Staples: Italian seasoning, garlic salt, ground black pepper
Hands-On Time: 15 minutes
Cook Time: 35 minutes

Serves 6

1 pound 80/20 ground beef
1 pound ground pork
3 large eggs, lightly beaten
1 cup panko bread crumbs
½ cup tomato sauce
1 tablespoon Italian seasoning
1 teaspoon garlic salt
½ teaspoon ground black pepper
1 cup water

HOMEMADE BREAD CRUMBS

If you don't have bread crumbs in the pantry, make your own! Simply cube whatever bread you have on hand, place it in a food processor, and pulse until desired consistency is reached. Add a layer of the pulsed bread to a baking sheet lined with parchment paper and bake 6 minutes at 350°F. Stir. Bake an additional 6 minutes, and they are ready.

1 In a large bowl, combine all ingredients (except water) with your hands.

2 Form mixture into a ball, flattening the top, then place meatloaf in a 7-cup glass baking dish.

3 Add water to the Instant Pot® and insert steam rack. Place glass baking dish on top of steam rack. Lock lid.

4 Press the Meat button and cook for the default of 35 minutes. When timer beeps, release pressure naturally for 10 minutes. Quick-release any additional pressure until float valve drops. Unlock lid.

5 Remove meatloaf from pot and let cool at room temperature 10 minutes. Gently tilt glass bowl and pour out and discard any liquid. Slice meatloaf and serve warm.

PER SERVING:

CALORIES: 382 | FAT: 19g | PROTEIN: 32g | SODIUM: 574mg | FIBER: 0g | CARBOHYDRATES: 15g | NET CARBS: 15g | SUGAR: 1g

Dry-Rubbed Baby Back Ribs

Dry rubs can bring just as much flavor as sauces, so don't be afraid to use the rub. Literally rub and massage the seasonings into the surface and grooves of the ribs. But brushing the ribs with a little sauce right before serving probably won't bring much controversy!

Pantry Staples: garlic salt, ground black pepper, olive oil
Hands-On Time: 10 minutes
Cook Time: 25 minutes

Serves 4

1 teaspoon garlic salt
1 teaspoon chili powder
1 teaspoon ground black pepper
½ teaspoon ground mustard
½ teaspoon onion powder
1 teaspoon instant espresso coffee
2 racks (about 3 pounds) pork baby back ribs, cut into 2-rib sections
2 cups water
1 tablespoon olive oil

1 In a small bowl, combine garlic salt, chili powder, pepper, ground mustard, onion powder, and espresso coffee. Massage mixture into rib sections. Refrigerate covered at least 1 hour or up to overnight.

2 Add water to the Instant Pot® and insert steam rack. Place steamer basket on top. Place ribs standing upright in basket with meaty side facing outward toward pot wall. Lock lid.

3 Press the Manual or Pressure Cook button and adjust time to 25 minutes. When timer beeps, let pressure release naturally until float valve drops. Unlock lid.

4 Transfer ribs to a platter and drizzle with oil. Serve warm.

PER SERVING:

CALORIES: 724 | FAT: 45g | PROTEIN: 62g | SODIUM: 693mg | FIBER: 0g | CARBOHYDRATES: 2g | NET CARBS: 2g | SUGAR: 0g

Juicy Pork Chops

These pork chops are so easy to make and taste delicious served with Mashed Sweet Potatoes (see recipe in Chapter 6) and/or Cinnamon Applesauce (see recipe in Chapter 11).

Pantry Staples: salt, ground black pepper, olive oil
Hands-On Time: 10 minutes
Cook Time: 11 minutes

Serves 2

1 large egg
1 cup cornmeal
1 teaspoon smoked paprika
1 teaspoon salt
½ teaspoon ground black pepper
2 (1"-thick) bone-in pork chops
2 tablespoons olive oil
1 cup water

1 In a small bowl, whisk egg. In a second small bowl, combine cornmeal, paprika, salt, and pepper.

2 Dip each pork chop in whisked egg and then dredge in cornmeal mixture. Set aside.

3 Press the Sauté button on the Instant Pot® and heat oil. Place pork chops in pot and brown 2–3 minutes on each side until browned. Press the Cancel button. Remove pork chops.

4 Add water to the Instant Pot® and insert steamer basket. Place pork chops in basket. Lock lid.

5 Press the Steam button and adjust time to 3 minutes. When timer beeps, let pressure release naturally for 5 minutes. Quick-release any additional pressure until float valve drops. Unlock lid.

6 While pressure is releasing, preheat oven to broiler for 500°F. Line a baking sheet with parchment paper.

7 Transfer pork chops to prepared baking sheet. Broil 2 minutes until tops are browned. Remove from heat and serve.

PER SERVING:

CALORIES: 529 | **FAT:** 15g | **PROTEIN:** 57g | **SODIUM:** 1,085mg | **FIBER:** 4g | **CARBOHYDRATES:** 36g | **NET CARBS:** 32g | **SUGAR:** 0g

Pulled Pork

A full boneless pork shoulder, or *pork butt*, as it is often called, weighs 6–9 pounds. It is also sold in half portions (3–4 pounds) in some grocery stores. If not, your butcher can help get you the right size, or you can simply cut one shoulder in half, prep both portions, and freeze what you don't use.

Pantry Staples: salt, ground black pepper, olive oil, beef broth
Hands-On Time: 15 minutes
Cook Time: 70 minutes

Serves 8

½ (4-pound) boneless pork shoulder, quartered
2 teaspoons salt
1 teaspoon ground black pepper
2 tablespoons olive oil
2 cups beef broth

THE MANY PERSONALITIES OF PORK

The great thing about cooking pork butt with simple seasonings is that you can tailor each leftover meal afterward. Mix in your favorite barbecue sauce with some of the pork and add it to a bun. Stir-fry some of the pork with sesame oil and your favorite vegetables for a little Asian flair. Or add some to your morning potato hash with a poached egg on top.

1 Season all sides of pork with salt and pepper.

2 Press the Sauté button on the Instant Pot® and heat oil. Place pork in pot. Sear meat for 5 minutes, making sure to get each side.

3 Add broth to pot. Press the Cancel button. Lock lid.

4 Press the Manual or Pressure Cook button and adjust time to 65 minutes. When timer beeps, let pressure release naturally for 10 minutes. Quick-release any additional pressure until float valve drops. Unlock lid.

5 Remove a few ladles of liquid from pot, as most is just fat rendered from pork.

6 Using two forks, shred pork and incorporate juices. Remove any additional unwanted liquid. Serve warm.

PER SERVING:

CALORIES: 217 | FAT: 14g | PROTEIN: 19g | SODIUM: 714mg | FIBER: 0g | CARBOHYDRATES: 0g | NET CARBS: 0g | SUGAR: 0g

Seasoned Boneless Pork Loin

This succulent cut of meat is a pretty inexpensive cut that can be enhanced by whatever flavors you add. Luckily, even seasoned with just salt and pepper, the flavor of pork still sings. Add some herbs and Parmesan, and this meal just stepped up.

Pantry Staples: salt, ground black pepper, Italian seasoning, all-purpose flour, olive oil
Hands-On Time: 10 minutes
Cook Time: 14 minutes

Serves 4

- 1 teaspoon salt
- 1 teaspoon ground black pepper
- 1 teaspoon Italian seasoning
- 2 tablespoons all-purpose flour
- 1 tablespoon grated Parmesan cheese
- 2 (6-ounce) boneless pork loin chops
- 2 tablespoons olive oil
- 1 cup water

1 In a large bowl, combine salt, pepper, Italian seasoning, flour, and cheese. Coat chops in mixture. Set aside.

2 Press the Sauté button on the Instant Pot® and heat oil. Add chops to pot and sear 2 minutes on each side, for a total of 8 minutes. Press the Cancel button. Remove pork from pot and set aside.

3 Pour water into the Instant Pot®. Place chops in steamer basket and insert into pot. Lock lid.

4 Press the Manual or Pressure Cook button and adjust time to 6 minutes. When timer beeps, quick-release pressure until float valve drops. Unlock lid.

5 Transfer chops to a cutting board. Let rest 5 minutes before slicing. Serve warm.

PER SERVING:

CALORIES: 178 | FAT: 8g | PROTEIN: 21g | SODIUM: 665mg |
FIBER: 1g | CARBOHYDRATES: 4g | NET CARBS: 3g | SUGAR: 0g

Pork Egg Roll in a Bowl

This is a meal that you'll make over and over again. Buy yourself a pretty bowl and a cool set of chopsticks, because I guarantee you that this will be a repeat meal. Sriracha is the recommended hot sauce for this recipe.

Pantry Staples: olive oil, hot sauce, garlic salt, chicken broth
Hands-On Time: 10 minutes
Cook Time: 7 minutes

Serves 4

1 tablespoon olive oil
1 pound ground pork
1 (14-ounce) bag coleslaw mix (cabbage and carrots)
¼ cup soy sauce
1 tablespoon hot sauce
2 teaspoons minced fresh ginger
½ teaspoon garlic salt
2 teaspoons rice wine vinegar
½ cup chicken broth

1 Press the Sauté button on the Instant Pot® and heat oil. Add pork and stir-fry 4 minutes until pork starts to brown.

2 Place remaining ingredients in pot. Press the Cancel button. Lock lid.

3 Press the Manual or Pressure Cook button and adjust time to 3 minutes. When timer beeps, quick-release pressure until float valve drops. Unlock lid.

4 Using a slotted spoon, transfer to serving bowls. Serve warm.

PER SERVING:

CALORIES: 311 | FAT: 19g | PROTEIN: 23g | SODIUM: 1,387mg | FIBER: 3g | CARBOHYDRATES: 7g | NET CARBS: 4g | SUGAR: 3g

9

Seafood and Fish Main Dishes

Seafood is one of those meals that gets ordered a lot at restaurants but is often overlooked at home. A lot of home chefs are timid when it comes to cooking fish and shellfish, but that's a shame. Fish and shellfish are not only low in calories and full of nutrients, but they are also some of the quickest meals you can cook in your Instant Pot®. In addition, the steaming functionality of the appliance makes for tender and moist meals.

The Instant Pot® easily and perfectly cooks your seafood with its steam and pressure capabilities. The recipes in this chapter call for short cooking times and quick pressure releases. You don't want to do a natural pressure release with most fish, as it will continue to cook if the pressure releases slowly. From Beer-Steamed Shrimp to Pistachio-Parm–Crusted Cod, this chapter covers a variety of delicious recipes and types of fish and seafood that will have you eating out of the water on a regular basis.

Shrimp Fajitas

This is a great meal to enjoy while standing around the kitchen island with the family and catching up on the busy day. Each fajita can be personalized with the addition of a fajita bar, where you can offer guacamole, sour cream, fresh cilantro, and even diced tomatoes. The Instant Pot® does the cooking, and the family does the assembly. Win-win!

Pantry Staples: none
Hands-On Time: 15 minutes
Cook Time: 0 minutes

Serves 8

- 2 pounds jumbo shrimp, peeled and deveined
- 2 medium bell peppers (color of choice), seeded and sliced
- 1 medium red onion, peeled and sliced
- 1 (8-ounce) packet fajita sauce
- 2 cups water
- 16 (6") flour tortillas, warmed

HOW TO WARM TORTILLAS IN THE MICROWAVE

Tortillas will often be a little dry and stiff from sitting on the shelves in the grocery store. To soften and warm them up, simply layer a damp paper towel between tortillas and microwave on high about 30 seconds.

1 In a medium bowl, add shrimp, bell peppers, onion, and fajita sauce. Refrigerate covered 30 minutes.

2 Add water to the Instant Pot® and insert steamer basket. Place shrimp and vegetables in basket. Lock lid.

3 Press the Steam button and adjust time to 0 minutes. When timer beeps, quick-release pressure until float valve drops. Unlock lid.

4 Transfer shrimp and vegetables to a serving bowl. Distribute mixture evenly on tortillas. Serve warm.

PER SERVING:

CALORIES: 275 | FAT: 4g | PROTEIN: 21g | SODIUM: 1,302mg | FIBER: 2g | CARBOHYDRATES: 36g | NET CARBS: 34g | SUGAR: 5g

Beer-Steamed Shrimp

You'll feel like you're sitting on the beach in the Carolinas with this dish. If you don't want to use beer, simply swap it out with some broth. Otherwise, kick back and enjoy this shrimp with some melted butter or cocktail sauce!

Pantry Staples: none
Hands-On Time: 5 minutes
Cook Time: 0 minutes

Serves 4

1 (12-ounce) bottle beer
2 pounds jumbo shrimp, peeled and deveined
1 medium lemon, quartered
2 tablespoons Old Bay Seasoning

1   Add beer to the Instant Pot® and insert steamer basket. Place shrimp in basket. Squeeze lemons over shrimp and add squeezed wedges for additional aromatics. Lock lid.

2   Press the Steam button and adjust time to 0 minutes. When timer beeps, quick-release pressure until float valve drops. Unlock lid. Discard lemons.

3   Transfer shrimp to a serving dish and toss with Old Bay Seasoning. Serve warm or chilled.

PER SERVING:

CALORIES: 163 | **FAT:** 2g | **PROTEIN:** 31g | **SODIUM:** 2,123mg | **FIBER:** 0g | **CARBOHYDRATES:** 3g | **NET CARBS:** 3g | **SUGAR:** 0g

Stewed Cod and Peppers

Stewing fish does not necessarily result in a soup or stew; however, this method helps infuse flavors into your fillet. Cod is an excellent vessel for this cooking process because it is a solid whitefish that can withstand the cooking liquid and soak up the flavors.

Pantry Staples: chicken broth, garlic salt, ground black pepper
Hands-On Time: 5 minutes
Cook Time: 3 minutes

Serves 2

- 1 (14.5-ounce) can fire-roasted diced tomatoes, including juice
- ½ cup chicken broth
- 2 teaspoons smoked paprika
- 1 medium green bell pepper, seeded and diced small
- ½ cup diced yellow onion
- 1 teaspoon garlic salt
- ¼ teaspoon ground black pepper
- 1 pound cod fillets, cut into bite-sized pieces

1. Place all ingredients except cod in the Instant Pot® and stir. Once mixed, add fish on top. Lock lid.

2. Press the Manual or Pressure Cook button and adjust time to 3 minutes. When timer beeps, quick-release pressure until float valve drops. Unlock lid.

3. Transfer to bowls. Serve warm.

PER SERVING:

CALORIES: 234 | FAT: 1g | PROTEIN: 38g | SODIUM: 2,302mg | FIBER: 6g | CARBOHYDRATES: 18g | NET CARBS: 12g | SUGAR: 9g

Calamari Poppers

There is more to calamari than just cutting them into little rings and deep-frying them. The bodies of calamari make the perfect little casings for whatever filler you can think of!

Pantry Staples: ground black pepper
Hands-On Time: 15 minutes
Cook Time: 3 minutes

Serves 4

10–12 calamari tubes
1 cup shredded sharp Cheddar cheese
¾ cup cream cheese, softened
¼ teaspoon garlic powder
¼ teaspoon ground black pepper
2 medium jalapeño peppers, seeded and diced
1 cup water

1 Rinse calamari tubes and set aside.

2 In a medium bowl, combine Cheddar cheese, cream cheese, garlic powder, black pepper, and jalapeños. Transfer mixture to a piping bag or plastic bag. Cut the tip off large enough for the mixture to pass through. Pipe cheese mixture into calamari tubes. Fasten opening of each calamari tube with a toothpick.

3 Add water to the Instant Pot® and insert steamer basket. Place stuffed calamari in an even row in basket. Lock lid.

4 Press the Manual or Pressure Cook button and adjust time to 3 minutes. When timer beeps, quick-release pressure until float valve drops. Unlock lid.

5 Transfer calamari to a plate. Remove toothpicks. Serve warm.

PER SERVING:

CALORIES: 541 | FAT: 25g | PROTEIN: 59g | SODIUM: 478mg | FIBER: 0g | CARBOHYDRATES: 11g | NET CARBS: 11g | SUGAR: 2g

Halibut with Lemon-Caper Sauce

This is such a humble fish served with a most elegant sauce. It is definitely date night–worthy; consider serving with a side of steamed asparagus.

Pantry Staples: salt, ground black pepper, chicken broth
Hands-On Time: 5 minutes
Cook Time: 12 minutes

Serves 4

Halibut

4 (5-ounce) halibut fillets
½ teaspoon salt
½ teaspoon ground black pepper
1 cup water

Sauce

2 tablespoons unsalted butter
1 medium shallot, peeled and diced
¼ cup chicken broth
⅛ teaspoon salt
2 tablespoons drained capers
Zest and juice of ½ medium lemon

---

1 Pat halibut fillets dry with a paper towel. Season with salt and pepper.

2 Add water to the Instant Pot®. Place fillets in steamer basket and insert into pot. Lock lid.

3 Press the Manual or Pressure Cook button and adjust time to 5 minutes. When timer beeps, quick-release pressure until float valve drops. Press the Cancel button. Unlock lid.

4 Line a baking sheet with parchment paper. Transfer fillets to prepared sheet. Broil fillets 2 minutes until tops are browned.

5 Empty water from the Instant Pot®, then press the Sauté button on pot. Add butter and heat until melted. Add shallot and stir-fry 2–3 minutes until tender. Add broth to deglaze pot. Add salt, capers, and zest and juice of lemon. Let cook an additional 2 minutes.

6 Transfer halibut to plates and top with sauce. Serve warm.

PER SERVING:

CALORIES: 186 | FAT: 7g | PROTEIN: 27g | SODIUM: 618mg | FIBER: 1g | CARBOHYDRATES: 2g | NET CARBS: 1g | SUGAR: 1g

Thyme for Lemon-Butter Sea Bass

Sea bass is mild, flaky whitefish similar to cod or haddock; however, it has an almost butter-like element that is unique to the fish. Because of its rich and delectable taste, you really don't have to add much for its flavor to shine.

Pantry Staples: salt, ground black pepper
Hands-On Time: 10 minutes
Cook Time: 7 minutes

Serves 2

2 tablespoons unsalted butter, melted
1 tablespoon lemon juice
2 teaspoons fresh thyme leaves
¼ cup Italian bread crumbs
2 (5-ounce) sea bass fillets
½ teaspoon salt
¼ teaspoon ground black pepper
1 cup water

1 In a small bowl, combine butter, lemon juice, thyme, and bread crumbs to form a thick paste.

2 Pat sea bass fillets dry with a paper towel. Season sea bass with salt and pepper. Press paste on top of each fillet and place in steamer basket.

3 Add water to the Instant Pot® and insert steam rack. Place basket on steam rack. Lock lid.

4 Press the Manual or Pressure Cook button and adjust time to 5 minutes. When timer beeps, quick-release pressure until float valve drops. Unlock lid.

5 Line a baking sheet with parchment paper. Transfer fillets to prepared baking sheet. Broil approximately 1–2 minutes until tops are browned.

6 Remove from heat. Serve warm.

PER SERVING:

CALORIES: 298 | **FAT:** 14g | **PROTEIN:** 28g | **SODIUM:** 878mg | **FIBER:** 1g | **CARBOHYDRATES:** 11g | **NET CARBS:** 10g | **SUGAR:** 1g

Pistachio-Parm–Crusted Cod

The mild, sweetish flavor of pistachios combined with the salty nature of Parmesan blends well on top of the mild-flavored cod. Low in calories but high in flavor, this dish is a winner.

Pantry Staples: salt
Hands-On Time: 5 minutes
Cook Time: 7 minutes

Serves 2

- 2 tablespoons unsalted butter, melted
- 1 tablespoon panko bread crumbs
- 2 tablespoons chopped unsalted pistachios
- 2 tablespoons grated Parmesan cheese
- ¼ teaspoon salt
- 2 (5-ounce) cod fillets
- 1 cup water

1 In a small bowl, combine butter, bread crumbs, pistachios, cheese, and salt to form a thick paste.

2 Pat cod fillets dry with a paper towel. Rub paste on top of each fillet and place in steamer basket.

3 Add water to the Instant Pot® and insert steam rack. Place steamer basket on steam rack. Lock lid.

4 Press the Manual or Pressure Cook button and adjust time to 5 minutes. When timer beeps, quick-release the pressure until float valve drops. Unlock lid.

5 Line a baking sheet with parchment paper. Transfer fillets to prepared baking sheet. Broil approximately 1–2 minutes until tops are browned.

6 Remove from heat and serve hot.

PER SERVING:

CALORIES: 275 | FAT: 16g | PROTEIN: 25g | SODIUM: 817mg | FIBER: 1g | CARBOHYDRATES: 5g | NET CARBS: 4g | SUGAR: 1g

Baja Fish Street Tacos

The flavors in each bite of these tacos—from the seasoned fish to the creamy, crunchy slaw—are heavenly. Your guests and family will think that you just ordered the best taco truck in the area to cater your meal.

Pantry Staples: olive oil, hot sauce, salt, ground black pepper
Hands-On Time: 15 minutes
Cook Time: 3 minutes

Serves 4

Slaw
½ cup grated red cabbage
2 medium limes (juice ½ lime for the slaw; cut the rest into wedges for garnish)
1 tablespoon olive oil
1 teaspoon hot sauce
1 tablespoon mayonnaise
½ teaspoon salt

Fish
1 pound cod, cubed
½ teaspoon salt
½ teaspoon ground black pepper
1 cup water

To Serve
8 (4.5") soft flour street taco tortillas, warmed

1 In a medium bowl, combine all slaw ingredients. Refrigerate covered 30 minutes or up to overnight.

2 In a large bowl, season fish with salt and pepper.

3 Add water to the Instant Pot and insert steam rack. Place steamer basket on top of steam rack. Add cod in an even row into basket. Lock lid.

4 Press the Manual or Pressure Cook button and adjust time to 3 minutes. When timer beeps, quick-release pressure until float valve drops. Unlock lid. Transfer fish to a serving dish.

5 Assemble fish tacos by adding equal amounts fish and slaw to each tortilla. Serve with lime wedges.

PER SERVING:

CALORIES: 285 | FAT: 10g | PROTEIN: 22g | SODIUM: 1,416mg | FIBER: 1g | CARBOHYDRATES: 27g | NET CARBS: 26g | SUGAR: 2g

Teriyaki Salmon

Cooking salmon—which is an oily fish and rich in protein and omega-3 fatty acids—in an Instant Pot® with a sweet teriyaki sauce creates a dish that is super tender and tasty.

Pantry Staples: salt
Hands-On Time: 5 minutes
Cook Time: 5 minutes

Serves 2

2 (5-ounce) salmon fillets
½ teaspoon salt
2 tablespoons teriyaki sauce
1 cup water
1 teaspoon toasted sesame seeds
2 tablespoons sliced green onion (greens only)

TOASTED SESAME SEEDS

Although sesame seeds can be purchased pre-toasted, it is an easy process to achieve by the home chef if you only have them in their raw form. Place an even layer of seeds on a baking sheet lined with parchment paper. Bake at 350°F for 8 minutes, stirring every 2 minutes so as not to let them burn. The result will be a lightly browned, nuttier, and crispier seed.

1 Pat fillets dry with a paper towel and place in a steamer basket. Season salmon with salt. Brush teriyaki sauce on tops of salmon.

2 Add water to the Instant Pot® and insert steam rack. Place steamer basket on steam rack. Lock lid.

3 Press the Manual or Pressure Cook button and adjust time to 5 minutes. When timer beeps, quick-release pressure until float valve drops. Unlock lid.

4 Transfer fish to plates and garnish with sesame seeds and onion greens. Serve immediately.

PER SERVING:

CALORIES: 225 | FAT: 9g | PROTEIN: 29g | SODIUM: 1,332mg | FIBER: 0g | CARBOHYDRATES: 3g | NET CARBS: 3g | SUGAR: 3g

Littleneck Clams in Garlic Wine Broth

Although these clams can stand alone as a dish, serving them over linguine with a side of crusty bread will take them up a notch. The bread can help sop up that beautiful broth. And you won't want to skip a drop.

Pantry Staples: olive oil, vegetable broth, salt
Hands-On Time: 10 minutes
Cook Time: 8 minutes

Serves 4

- 2 pounds fresh littleneck clams, cleaned and debearded
- 2 tablespoons olive oil
- 1 medium yellow onion, peeled and diced
- 4 cloves garlic, peeled and minced
- ½ cup dry white wine
- ½ cup vegetable broth
- ½ teaspoon salt
- 4 tablespoons chopped fresh parsley

PURGING CLAMS

Depending on how fresh your clams are, most have already been through at least one purging process. Soaking your clams again in water at least 30 minutes ensures that they purge any other additional impurities and sand particles still in the shells. Throwing a scattering of cornmeal helps this process along.

1 Let clams soak in water 30 minutes. Rinse several times. This will help purge any sand trapped in the shells.

2 Press the Sauté button on the Instant Pot® and heat oil. Add onion and sauté 3–5 minutes until translucent. Add garlic and cook an additional 1 minute. Stir in wine, broth, and salt and let cook 2 minutes. Press the Cancel button.

3 Insert steamer basket. Place clams in basket. Lock lid.

4 Press the Manual or Pressure Cook button and adjust time to 0 minutes. When timer beeps, quick-release pressure until float valve drops. Unlock lid.

5 Remove clams and discard any that haven't opened. Transfer clams to four bowls and pour liquid from the Instant Pot® equally among bowls. Garnish each bowl with 1 tablespoon parsley. Serve immediately.

PER SERVING:

CALORIES: 118 | **FAT:** 7g | **PROTEIN:** 6g | **SODIUM:** 598mg | **FIBER:** 1g | **CARBOHYDRATES:** 6g | **NET CARBS:** 5g | **SUGAR:** 2g

Mussels with Chorizo and Tomato Broth

Mussels are such an underused ingredient on most of our weekly menus, but they shouldn't be. The bang for the buck is exceptional. They are inexpensive, easy to prepare, and extremely nutritious. The added chorizo and tomatoes in this recipe provide a little Mediterranean flair and a bit of a kick.

Pantry Staples: olive oil, chicken broth
Hands-On Time: 10 minutes
Cook Time: 11 minutes

Serves 4

- 2 tablespoons olive oil
- 1 medium yellow onion, peeled and diced
- ½ pound chorizo, loose or removed from casings
- 1½ cups chicken broth
- 1 (14.5-ounce) can diced tomatoes, including juice
- 2 pounds fresh mussels, cleaned and debearded
- 4 tablespoons chopped fresh parsley

DEBEARDING MUSSELS

Most commercial mussels will come with the beard already removed. But, if you are buying fresh, they can sometimes still be attached. Pinch the visible threads between your thumb and index finger and give it a tug. There are also plenty of online videos to help you out if you need a visual.

1 Press the Sauté button on the Instant Pot® and heat oil. Add onion and sauté 3–5 minutes until translucent. Add chorizo. Stir-fry 3–4 minutes until chorizo is browned. Stir in broth and let cook 2 minutes, then add tomatoes. Press the Cancel button.

2 Insert steamer basket and place mussels in basket. Lock lid.

3 Press the Manual or Pressure Cook button and adjust time to 0 minutes. When timer beeps, quick-release pressure until float valve drops. Unlock lid.

4 Remove mussels and discard any that haven't opened. Transfer mussels to four bowls and pour liquid from the Instant Pot® equally among bowls. Garnish each bowl with 1 tablespoon parsley. Serve immediately.

PER SERVING:

CALORIES: 409 | FAT: 28g | PROTEIN: 22g | SODIUM: 1,398mg | FIBER: 2g | CARBOHYDRATES: 11g | NET CARBS: 9g | SUGAR: 4g

Chilled Lobster Salad

This salad is so versatile. Scoop into a bowl, serve in lettuce wraps, or load onto a top-split bun, or even top with a beautiful poached egg for a decadent breakfast. Don't forget the mimosas!

Pantry Staples: hot sauce, salt, ground black pepper
Hands-On Time: 2 minutes
Cook Time: 4 minutes

Serves 4

- 1 cup water
- 4 (6-ounce) lobster tails, thawed
- ¼ cup mayonnaise
- 1 medium stalk celery, diced
- Juice and zest from ½ medium lemon
- ¼ teaspoon hot sauce
- ½ teaspoon salt
- ¼ teaspoon ground black pepper
- 2 medium avocados, peeled, pitted, and diced

1 Add water to the Instant Pot® and insert steamer basket. Add lobster tails to basket. Lock lid.

2 Press the Steam button and adjust time to 4 minutes. When timer beeps, quick-release pressure until float valve drops. Unlock lid. Transfer tails to an ice bath (1 cup ice and 1 cup water), to stop lobster from overcooking.

3 Remove lobster meat from shells. Roughly chop meat and transfer to a medium bowl. Combine lobster with mayonnaise, celery, lemon juice and zest, hot sauce, salt, and pepper.

4 Refrigerate until ready to serve. Spoon salad into bowls and garnish with avocado. Serve.

PER SERVING:

CALORIES: 340 | FAT: 21g | PROTEIN: 30g | SODIUM: 1,119mg | FIBER: 5g | CARBOHYDRATES: 7g | NET CARBS: 2g | SUGAR: 1g

Orange Roughy with Zucchini

This dish has a little bit of this and a little bit of that. This delicious low-carb meal is made for a person with an overproducing garden!

Pantry Staples: salt, ground black pepper
Hands-On Time: 10 minutes
Cook Time: 3 minutes

Serves 2

1 cup water
1 large zucchini, thinly sliced
2 (6-ounce) orange roughy fillets, cubed
Juice of 1 medium lemon
1 teaspoon salt
½ teaspoon ground black pepper
4 tablespoons unsalted butter, cut into 8 pats
2 tablespoons chopped fresh parsley

1 Add water to the Instant Pot® and insert steamer basket.

2 Add zucchini to basket in an even layer. Add orange roughy fillets on top. Squeeze lemon juice over fish. Season with salt and pepper. Distribute butter pats on fish and zucchini. Lock lid.

3 Press the Manual or Pressure Cook button and adjust time to 3 minutes. When timer beeps, quick-release pressure until float valve drops. Unlock lid.

4 Transfer fish and zucchini to two plates. Garnish with parsley. Serve warm.

PER SERVING:

CALORIES: 363 | FAT: 22g | PROTEIN: 30g | SODIUM: 1,302mg | FIBER: 2g | CARBOHYDRATES: 6g | NET CARBS: 4g | SUGAR: 4g

Lobster Lettuce Wraps

This classic New England dish can be yours in minutes with your Instant Pot®. The lobster meat shines with very few seasonings. While it is traditionally served on a top-split buttered hot dog bun, this carb-conscious version is just as delicious!

Pantry Staples: salt, ground black pepper
Hands-On Time: 2 minutes
Cook Time: 4 minutes

Serves 4

1 cup water
4 (6-ounce) lobster tails, thawed
¼ cup mayonnaise
1 medium stalk celery, diced
Juice and zest from ½ large lemon
½ teaspoon salt
¼ teaspoon ground black pepper
1 head Bibb lettuce

1 Add water to the Instant Pot® and insert steamer basket. Add lobster tails to basket. Lock lid.

2 Press the Steam button and adjust time to 4 minutes. When timer beeps, quick-release pressure until float valve drops. Unlock lid. Transfer tails to an ice bath (1 cup water plus 1 cup ice) to stop lobster from overcooking.

3 Remove lobster meat from shells. Roughly chop meat and transfer to a medium bowl.

4 Combine lobster with mayonnaise, celery, lemon juice and zest, salt, and pepper.

5 Distribute lobster mixture among lettuce leaves. Serve warm or chilled.

PER SERVING:

CALORIES: 232 | FAT: 11g | PROTEIN: 29g | SODIUM: 1,107mg | FIBER: 1g | CARBOHYDRATES: 2g | NET CARBS: 1g | SUGAR: 1g

Crab Risotto

This is absolutely a date night meal. It's rich and creamy and decadent! Don't skimp on the crabmeat here. Go for the good stuff! And with the Instant Pot® doing all of the work, you'll have more time to get ready and open that bottle of wine.

Pantry Staples: vegetable broth, garlic salt, ground black pepper
Hands-On Time: 10 minutes
Cook Time: 15 minutes

Serves 4

- 4 tablespoons unsalted butter
- 1 small yellow onion, peeled and finely diced
- 1½ cups Arborio rice
- 4 cups vegetable broth
- 3 tablespoons grated Parmesan cheese, divided
- ½ teaspoon garlic salt
- ¼ teaspoon ground black pepper
- 1 cup lump crabmeat, picked over for shells

ADD IT IN!

To freshen up this lovely dish, garnish the finished product with some chopped fresh parsley and a little lemon zest. It's like putting a little lipstick on an already beautiful face!

1 Press the Sauté button on the Instant Pot®. Add butter and heat until melted. Add onion and stir-fry 3–5 minutes until translucent.

2 Add rice, broth, 2 tablespoons cheese, garlic salt, and pepper. Press the Cancel button. Lock lid.

3 Press the Manual or Pressure Cook button and adjust time to 10 minutes. When timer beeps, let pressure release naturally for 10 minutes. Quick-release any additional pressure until float valve drops. Unlock lid.

4 Stir in crab and remaining cheese. Serve warm.

PER SERVING:

CALORIES: 431 | FAT: 12g | PROTEIN: 12g | SODIUM: 1,305mg | FIBER: 2g | CARBOHYDRATES: 64g | NET CARBS: 62g | SUGAR: 3g

Thai-Inspired Poached Salmon

Although crispy fish can certainly be a treat, poaching it is just as desirable. It results in a moist, tender, and flaky fillet because there is little loss of moisture during the cooking process. Sriracha is the recommended hot sauce for this recipe.

Pantry Staples: hot sauce, salt
Hands-On Time: 5 minutes
Cook Time: 3 minutes

Serves 4

1 (13.5-ounce) can coconut milk

Juice and zest of 1 medium lime

1 teaspoon lemongrass paste

1 tablespoon hot sauce

½ teaspoon salt

4 (4-ounce) salmon fillets

½ cup fresh basil chiffonade, divided

WHAT IS LEMONGRASS PASTE?

Lemongrass paste is exactly what it sounds like: lemongrass that has been prewashed, chopped, and tubed for your convenience. It can be found in the produce section of most grocery stores. If you can't find this, by all means, use the fresh stuff!

1 In the Instant Pot®, whisk together coconut milk, lime juice and zest, lemongrass paste, hot sauce, and salt. Add salmon and ¼ cup basil. Lock lid.

2 Press the Manual or Pressure Cook button and adjust time to 3 minutes. When timer beeps, quick-release pressure until float valve drops. Unlock lid.

3 Transfer fish and broth to bowls and garnish with remaining basil. Serve warm.

PER SERVING:

CALORIES: 355 | FAT: 26g | PROTEIN: 25g | SODIUM: 510mg | FIBER: 0g | CARBOHYDRATES: 4g | NET CARBS: 4g | SUGAR: 0g

Creamed Crab Sauce

Date night alert! This Creamed Crab Sauce is excellent served over a nice steak or grilled asparagus. You can even use a nice crusty artisanal bread to sop up this dreamy, rich sauce.

Pantry Staples: chicken broth, all-purpose flour, salt, ground black pepper

Hands-On Time: 5 minutes

Cook Time: 5 minutes

Serves 4

2 tablespoons unsalted butter

¼ cup finely diced red onion

1 pound lump crabmeat

¼ cup chicken broth

6 ounces cream cheese, softened

2 teaspoons cooking sherry

1 tablespoon all-purpose flour

½ teaspoon salt

½ teaspoon ground black pepper

1. Press the Sauté button on the Instant Pot®. Add butter and heat until melted. Add onion; stir-fry 3–5 minutes until onions begin to soften.

2. Stir crabmeat and broth into pot. Press the Cancel button. Lock lid.

3. Press the Steam button on the Instant Pot® and adjust time to 0 minutes. When timer beeps, quick-release pressure until float valve drops. Unlock lid.

4. Stir in cream cheese, sherry, flour, salt, and pepper. Transfer to a serving bowl. Let sit 10 minutes to thicken. Serve warm.

PER SERVING:

CALORIES: 303 | FAT: 19g | PROTEIN: 23g | SODIUM: 1,157mg | FIBER: 0g | CARBOHYDRATES: 5g | NET CARBS: 5g | SUGAR: 2g

WHAT KIND OF CRAB SHOULD YOU CHOOSE?

Fresh lump crabmeat is the best option for this recipe—but it can be pricey. Fortunately, there are many different varieties and sections of the crab that can be purchased at a lower price. It is even sold in cans. Although there is imitation "krab" available, draw the line at that. It is stringy and packed with starch and chemicals.

10

Vegetarian Main Dishes

This chapter is specifically written for vegetarians. But, don't overlook these recipes if you don't consider yourself in this group. Maybe you are vegetarian-curious. Maybe you just partake in Meatless Mondays. Maybe you just like good food. Even within the vegetarian community, there are many different personalities. Whether you are a vegan, vegetarian, lacto-vegetarian, lacto-ovo vegetarian, only-on-the-weekends vegetarian... see what I mean? Just as a "no-carb" diet actually receives carbohydrates from certain vegetables, vegetarians get protein from beans, quinoa, and other ingredients. From Easy Cheesy Mac, Tortellini in Brodo, and Cauliflower Charcuterie, this chapter covers a variety of drool-worthy vegetarian recipes.

Orzo Pilaf

Although toasting your orzo is not necessary, it lends an earthy nuttiness to the dish. It is a simple step that really enhances the flavor.

Pantry Staples: olive oil, vegetable broth, salt
Hands-On Time: 5 minutes
Cook Time: 7 minutes

Serves 4

1 tablespoon olive oil
½ medium yellow onion, peeled and diced small
1 cup orzo
1 cup vegetable broth
½ teaspoon salt
¼ cup chopped fresh parsley

1 Press the Sauté button on the Instant Pot® and heat oil. Add onion and orzo. Stir-fry 3–4 minutes until orzo is browned. Add broth and salt. Press the Cancel button. Lock lid.

2 Press the Manual or Pressure Cook button and adjust time to 3 minutes. When timer beeps, quick-release pressure until float valve drops. Unlock lid.

3 Transfer orzo to a medium bowl and toss in parsley. Serve warm.

PER SERVING:

CALORIES: 189 | FAT: 4g | PROTEIN: 6g | SODIUM: 493mg | FIBER: 2g | CARBOHYDRATES: 34g | NET CARBS: 32g | SUGAR: 3g

Easy Cheesy Mac

Depending on where you fall on the spectrum of vegetarian or vegan, there are many substitutions available. Vegan cheese has improved tremendously, with its yummy gooeyness mimicking "real" cheese, so feel free to substitute it in this dish if you desire.

Pantry Staples: salt, ground black pepper
Hands-On Time: 5 minutes
Cook Time: 4 minutes

Serves 4

1 pound elbow macaroni
¼ cup unsweetened almond milk
1 cup shredded sharp Cheddar cheese
½ cup ricotta cheese
2 tablespoons unsalted butter
1 teaspoon salt
½ teaspoon ground black pepper

1 Place macaroni in an even layer in the Instant Pot®. Pour enough water to come about ¼" over pasta. Lock lid.

2 Press the Manual or Pressure Cook button and adjust time to 4 minutes. When timer beeps, let pressure release naturally for 3 minutes. Quick-release any additional pressure until float valve drops. Unlock lid.

3 Drain any residual water. Add remaining ingredients. Stir in warmed pot until well combined. Serve warm.

PER SERVING:

CALORIES: 718 | FAT: 20g | PROTEIN: 29g | SODIUM: 804mg | FIBER: 6g | CARBOHYDRATES: 99g | NET CARBS: 93g | SUGAR: 2g

Tortellini in Brodo

Brodo literally means "broth." This traditional Italian menu item uses a little broth, vegetables, and tortellini to create a simply delicious bowl.

Pantry Staples: olive oil, vegetable broth, salt, ground black pepper

Hands-On Time: 10 minutes

Cook Time: 15 minutes

Serves 4

- 1 tablespoon olive oil
- 1 small yellow onion, peeled and diced
- 1 large carrot, peeled and diced small
- 1 medium stalk celery, diced
- 1 (12-ounce) package dried three-cheese tortellini
- 4 cups vegetable broth
- ½ teaspoon salt
- ½ teaspoon ground black pepper
- 1 cup baby spinach

1 Press the Sauté button on the Instant Pot® and heat oil. Stir-fry onion, carrot, and celery 3–5 minutes until onions are translucent.

2 Add tortellini, broth, salt, and pepper. Press the Cancel button. Lock lid.

3 Press the Manual or Pressure Cook button and adjust time to 10 minutes. When timer beeps, let pressure release naturally for 5 minutes. Quick-release any additional pressure until float valve drops. Unlock lid. Add baby spinach and stir until wilted.

4 Ladle portions into bowls. Serve warm.

PER SERVING:

CALORIES: 361 | FAT: 14g | PROTEIN: 13g | SODIUM: 1,663mg | FIBER: 7g | CARBOHYDRATES: 53g | NET CARBS: 46g | SUGAR: 7g

ADD IT IN!

This "brothy" goodness is excellent garnished with freshly grated vegetarian Parmigiano-Reggiano. And did you ever wonder how to use that rind that is leftover? This is a perfect soup to use it in. Just like a bay leaf, it can be used during the cooking process to lend even more flavor. Simply discard after use.

Black Bean Slider Patties

The Instant Pot® was made to cook beans. These patties are delicious for a group or simply as meal prep for the week. They pack a punch and can be eaten alongside a salad or rice, or even on a slider bun drizzled with some Sriracha Aioli (see recipe in sidebar)!

Pantry Staples: olive oil, vegetable broth, salt, ground black pepper
Hands-On Time: 10 minutes
Cook Time: 49 minutes

Serves 8

1 tablespoon olive oil
1 small red bell pepper, seeded and diced small
2 cups vegetable broth
1 cup dried black beans, rinsed and drained
2 teaspoons chili powder
½ teaspoon salt
½ teaspoon ground black pepper
1 large egg
1 cup panko bread crumbs

CHEATER SRIRACHA AIOLI

Aioli, in a nutshell, is flavored mayonnaise. You don't have to make it from scratch for it to be fancy. Whisk together 1 cup mayonnaise, 1 tablespoon sriracha, 2 minced garlic cloves, 1 tablespoon fresh lime juice, and a pinch or two of salt. Refrigerate overnight until ready to serve over the Black Bean Slider Patties.

1 Press the Sauté button on the Instant Pot® and heat oil. Add bell pepper and stir-fry 2–3 minutes until pepper is tender. Add broth and deglaze by scraping the bottom and sides of pot.

2 Add beans, chili powder, salt, and pepper. Press the Cancel button. Lock lid.

3 Press the Bean button and cook for the default time of 30 minutes. When timer beeps, let pressure release naturally for 10 minutes. Quick-release any additional pressure until float valve drops. Press the Cancel button. Unlock lid.

4 Press the Sauté button on the Instant Pot®, press the Adjust button to change the heat to Less, and simmer bean mixture unlidded 10 minutes to thicken. Transfer mixture to a large bowl.

5 Once bean mixture is cool enough to handle, quickly mix in egg and bread crumbs. Form into sixteen equal-sized small patties.

6 In a medium skillet over medium heat, cook patties approximately 2–3 minutes per side until browned. Serve warm.

PER SERVING:

CALORIES: 159 | FAT: 3g | PROTEIN: 7g | SODIUM: 403mg | FIBER: 4g | CARBOHYDRATES: 26g | NET CARBS: 22g | SUGAR: 2g

Tex-Mex Quinoa

Quinoa, although technically a grain, is considered a complete protein, meaning it contains all of the nine essential amino acids that our bodies don't produce on their own. Couple that with the antioxidants and thousands of trace nutrients, and quinoa is a powerhouse base to a variety of meals.

Pantry Staples: garlic salt, ground black pepper
Hands-On Time: 5 minutes
Cook Time: 20 minutes

Serves 4

1 cup quinoa
2 cups water
1 cup chunky salsa
1 cup corn kernels
1 cup canned black beans, drained and rinsed
1 teaspoon ground cumin
½ teaspoon garlic salt
¼ teaspoon ground black pepper

1 Add quinoa and water to the Instant Pot®. Stir well. Lock lid.

2 Press the Porridge button and cook for the default time of 20 minutes. When timer beeps, quick-release pressure until float valve drops. Unlock lid.

3 Stir in salsa, corn, beans, cumin, garlic salt, and pepper. Let rest in heated pot 5 minutes to warm.

4 Transfer quinoa to a serving dish and fluff with a fork. Serve warm.

PER SERVING:

CALORIES: 260 | FAT: 3g | PROTEIN: 11g | SODIUM: 849mg | FIBER: 10g | CARBOHYDRATES: 48g | NET CARBS: 38g | SUGAR: 6g

Quick Cassoulet

This French creation is a stew-like casserole containing vegetables and meat, traditionally pork. In this recipe, the pork is subbed out for vegan smoked sausages. Use your favorite brand of vegan or vegetarian smoked sausages in this one!

Pantry Staples: olive oil, Italian seasoning, garlic salt, ground black pepper, vegetable broth
Hands-On Time: 5 minutes
Cook Time: 45 minutes

Serves 6

1 tablespoon olive oil
1 medium yellow onion, peeled and diced
2 cups dried cannellini beans, rinsed and drained
2 medium carrots, peeled and diced small
1 tablespoon Italian seasoning
1 teaspoon garlic salt
½ teaspoon ground black pepper
2½ cups vegetable broth
1 (14.5-ounce) can diced tomatoes, including juice
4 vegan smoked apple sausages, each cut into 4 sections

1 Press the Sauté button on the Instant Pot® and heat oil. Add onion and stir-fry 3–5 minutes until onions are translucent. Add beans and toss.

2 Add carrots, Italian seasoning, garlic salt, and pepper.

3 Gently pour in broth and diced tomatoes. Press the Cancel button. Lock lid.

4 Press the Bean button and cook for the default time of 30 minutes. When timer beeps, let pressure release naturally for 10 minutes. Quick-release any additional pressure until float valve drops. Press the Cancel button. Unlock lid. Add sausage.

5 Press the Sauté button on the Instant Pot®, press the Adjust button to change the temperature to Less, and simmer bean mixture unlidded 10 minutes to thicken. Transfer to a serving bowl and carefully toss. Serve warm.

PER SERVING:

CALORIES: 407 | FAT: 7g | PROTEIN: 32g | SODIUM: 1,140mg | FIBER: 17g | CARBOHYDRATES: 55g | NET CARBS: 38g | SUGAR: 9g

Cauliflower Charcuterie

Why should meat eaters have all of the fun with those beautiful charcuterie trays? Make your own cauliflower version with flavored cauliflower bites and different sauces. Fill in the gaps on your tray with cut celery, carrots, peppers, cheese, breads, or whatever your heart desires. Gather round with friends for a unique dining experience! Frank's RedHot sauce is recommended for the hot sauce in this recipe.

Pantry Staples: hot sauce
Hands-On Time: 15 minutes
Cook Time: 2 minutes

Serves 4

¼ cup hot sauce
¼ cup teriyaki sauce
1 cup water
1 large head cauliflower, chopped into bite-sized florets
½ cup ranch dip
½ cup blue cheese dip
4 medium stalks celery, cut into 1″ sections

1 Add hot sauce to a medium bowl. Add teriyaki sauce to another medium bowl. Set aside.

2 Add water to the Instant Pot®. Add steamer basket to pot and add cauliflower in basket in an even layer. Lock lid.

3 Press the Manual or Pressure Cook button and adjust time to 2 minutes. When timer beeps, quick-release pressure until float valve drops. Unlock lid.

4 Transfer half of cauliflower to bowl with hot sauce and toss. Transfer other half of cauliflower to bowl with teriyaki sauce and toss. Serve warm with dipping sauces and celery.

PER SERVING:

CALORIES: 242 | FAT: 18g | PROTEIN: 6g | SODIUM: 1,431mg | FIBER: 5g | CARBOHYDRATES: 16g | NET CARBS: 11g | SUGAR: 7g

Cali Dogs

Feeling a little Hollywood today? Enjoy this twist on hot dog ingredients for a change of pace. The creaminess of the avocado and goat cheese are delicious on your dog, and the bean sprouts add a little welcomed crunch!

Pantry Staples: none
Hands-On Time: 10 minutes
Cook Time: 0 minutes

Serves 4

2 cups water
8 meat-free, plant-based hot dogs
8 hot dog buns
½ cup alfalfa sprouts
1 medium avocado, peeled, pitted, and diced
½ cup crumbled goat cheese

1 Pour water into the Instant Pot®. Add hot dogs. Lock lid.

2 Press the Manual or Pressure Cook button and adjust time to 0 minutes. When timer beeps, quick-release pressure until float valve drops. Unlock lid.

3 Assemble hot dogs by placing them in buns and topping with remaining ingredients. Serve warm.

PER SERVING:

CALORIES: 470 | FAT: 14g | PROTEIN: 28g | SODIUM: 1,393mg | FIBER: 6g | CARBOHYDRATES: 54g | NET CARBS: 48g | SUGAR: 9g

Sweet Potato Chili

This full-bodied, hearty chili will warm your soul on those cold nights after a long day. Top it off with your favorites such as plain Greek yogurt, fresh cilantro, or pickled jalapeños, or you can even crumble a handful of tortilla chips over the top of your bowl!

Pantry Staples: olive oil, hot sauce, garlic salt, vegetable broth
Hands-On Time: 10 minutes
Cook Time: 17 minutes

Serves 4

1 tablespoon olive oil
1 small yellow onion, peeled and diced
2 medium sweet potatoes, peeled and diced
1 (15-ounce) can kidney beans, drained and rinsed
2 tablespoons chili powder
1 tablespoon hot sauce
1 teaspoon garlic salt
1 (28-ounce) can fire-roasted diced tomatoes, including juice
2 cups vegetable broth

1 Press the Sauté button on the Instant Pot® and heat oil. Add onion. Stir-fry 3–5 minutes until onions are translucent.

2 Add remaining ingredients to pot and stir to combine. Press the Cancel button. Lock lid.

3 Press the Manual or Pressure Cook button and adjust time to 12 minutes. When timer beeps, let pressure release naturally until float valve drops. Unlock lid.

4 Ladle chili into bowls. Serve warm.

PER SERVING:

CALORIES: 242 | FAT: 4g | PROTEIN: 9g | SODIUM: 1,671mg | FIBER: 12g | CARBOHYDRATES: 42g | NET CARBS: 30g | SUGAR: 11g

Blood Orange and Goat Cheese Wheat Berry Salad

Wheat berries contain protein, fiber, and B_6 vitamins, making them a grain powerhouse. The sweetness of the cranberries, the nuttiness of the wheat berries, and the creaminess of the goat cheese will make you come back to this zippy salad again and again.

Pantry Staples: olive oil, salt
Hands-On Time: 15 minutes
Cook Time: 35 minutes

Serves 6

3 tablespoons olive oil, divided
1 cup wheat berries
2 cups water
½ cup dried cranberries
Juice and zest of ½ medium blood orange
1 tablespoon balsamic vinegar
½ teaspoon salt
¼ cup crumbled goat cheese

1 Press Sauté button on Instant Pot® and heat 1 tablespoon oil. Add wheat berries. Stir-fry 4–5 minutes until browned and fragrant. Add water. Press the Cancel button. Lock lid.

2 Press the Manual or Pressure Cook button and adjust time to 30 minutes. When timer beeps, let pressure release naturally for 10 minutes. Quick-release any additional pressure until float valve drops. Unlock lid.

3 Let cool 10 minutes and drain any additional liquid.

4 Transfer cooled berries to a medium bowl and add remaining ingredients, including remaining oil. Refrigerate covered. Serve chilled.

PER SERVING:

CALORIES: 235 | FAT: 9g | PROTEIN: 6g | SODIUM: 223mg | FIBER: 7g | CARBOHYDRATES: 32g | NET CARBS: 25g | SUGAR: 8g

Baby Bella Burgundy

Although Julia Child is known for her classic boeuf bourguignon, don't we all think that she would have cut some corners if she only had owned an Instant Pot®? This mushroom version is best served over a starchy base like egg noodles, potatoes, or rice.

Pantry Staples: olive oil, Italian seasoning, garlic salt, vegetable broth
Hands-On Time: 10 minutes
Cook Time: 17 minutes

Serves 4

4 tablespoons olive oil

3 medium shallots, peeled and diced

4 cups sliced baby bella mushrooms

1 cup dry red wine

2 medium carrots, peeled and thinly sliced

2 tablespoons Italian seasoning

1 teaspoon garlic salt

1 cup vegetable broth

2 tablespoons tomato paste

1 Press the Sauté button on the Instant Pot® and heat oil. Add shallots and mushrooms and cook 3–5 minutes until shallots are translucent.

2 Deglaze pot by adding red wine, scraping any bits from bottom and sides of pot. Cook an additional 2 minutes to allow alcohol to cook off.

3 Add carrots, Italian seasoning, garlic salt, broth, and tomato paste to pot. Press the Cancel button. Lock lid.

4 Press the Manual or Pressure Cook button and adjust time to 10 minutes. When timer beeps, quick-release pressure until float valve drops. Unlock lid.

5 Ladle mixture into bowls. Serve warm.

PER SERVING:

CALORIES: 187 | FAT: 13g | PROTEIN: 3g | SODIUM: 781mg | FIBER: 2g | CARBOHYDRATES: 11g | NET CARBS: 9g | SUGAR: 5g

Penne alla Mushroom "Bolognese"

Bolognese is an Italian meat sauce served over pasta. Because mushrooms have a certain meatiness to them, they are the perfect swap for the beef and/or pork traditionally used. And if you so choose, a little vegetarian Parmesan cheese sprinkled on top is a great addition.

Pantry Staples: olive oil, vegetable broth
Hands-On Time: 10 minutes
Cook Time: 9 minutes

Serves 6

1 tablespoon olive oil
1 medium yellow onion, peeled and diced
3 cups sliced white mushrooms
1 (45-ounce) jar marinara sauce
1 cup chopped fresh basil leaves, divided
1 pound penne pasta
½ cup vegetable broth

1 Press the Sauté button on the Instant Pot® and heat oil. Add onion and mushrooms and cook 3–5 minutes until onions are translucent. Add marinara sauce, ½ cup basil leaves, penne, and broth. Press the Cancel button. Lock lid.

2 Press the Manual or Pressure Cook button and adjust time to 4 minutes. When timer beeps, let pressure release naturally for 3 minutes. Quick-release any additional pressure until float valve drops. Unlock lid.

3 Transfer pasta to bowls. Garnish with remaining basil leaves. Serve warm.

PER SERVING:

CALORIES: 421 | FAT: 5g | PROTEIN: 14g | SODIUM: 964mg | FIBER: 7g | CARBOHYDRATES: 76g | NET CARBS: 69g | SUGAR: 15g

Curried Red Potatoes

The Instant Pot® makes this dish quick to fix, and there is no need to take the extra time to peel the potatoes. The red potatoes add not only optics to the dish but also fiber, vitamins, and minerals.

Pantry Staples: olive oil, garlic salt, ground black pepper, vegetable broth
Hands-On Time: 10 minutes
Cook Time: 20 minutes

Serves 6

- 1 tablespoon olive oil
- 1 small yellow onion, peeled and diced
- 3 pounds small red potatoes, quartered
- 2 tablespoons curry paste
- 1 teaspoon red chile flakes
- 1 teaspoon garlic salt
- 1 teaspoon ground black pepper
- 2 cups vegetable broth
- 2 tablespoons cornstarch

THE DIFFERENCE BETWEEN GREEN AND RED CURRY PASTE

Although either curry can be used in this dish, there are some slight differences, other than the obvious color difference. Red curry paste is slightly spicier because of the red chiles used. Green chiles are used for the green curry paste, and they lend a sweeter, milder flavor.

1. Press the Sauté button on the Instant Pot® and heat oil. Add onion. Stir-fry 3–5 minutes until onions are translucent.

2. Add potatoes, curry paste, red chile flakes, garlic salt, pepper, and broth to pot and stir to combine. Press the Cancel button. Lock lid.

3. Press the Manual or Pressure Cook button and adjust time to 15 minutes. When timer beeps, let pressure release naturally until float valve drops. Unlock lid.

4. Ladle a spoonful of liquid from pot into a small bowl. Whisk in cornstarch until smooth. Add this slurry back to pot and let sit 5 minutes until sauce thickens.

5. Ladle potatoes and sauce into bowls. Serve warm.

PER SERVING:

CALORIES: 204 | FAT: 3g | PROTEIN: 5g | SODIUM: 771mg | FIBER: 4g | CARBOHYDRATES: 42g | NET CARBS: 38g | SUGAR: 4g

Five-Can Minestrone

Have you ever had that day when life just doesn't seem to line up? You don't feel like cooking, but you are craving a healthy meal. This recipe couldn't be easier. Dump the ingredients in the pot, go get into comfy clothes, and come back to a finished meal!

Pantry Staples: vegetable broth
Hands-On Time: 5 minutes
Cook Time: 3 minutes

Serves 4

1 (14.5-ounce) can diced, fire-roasted tomatoes, including juice

1 (15.25-ounce) can sweet golden corn, drained

1 (14.5-ounce) can mixed vegetables

1 (15-ounce) can cannellini beans, drained and rinsed

1 (19-ounce) can minestrone soup

2 cups vegetable broth

1 Add all ingredients to the Instant Pot®. Lock lid.

2 Press the Manual button and adjust time to 3 minutes. When timer beeps, quick-release pressure until float valve drops. Unlock lid.

3 Ladle soup into bowls. Serve warm.

PER SERVING:

CALORIES: 251 | FAT: 1g | PROTEIN: 12g | SODIUM: 1,478mg | FIBER: 12g | CARBOHYDRATES: 47g | NET CARBS: 35g | SUGAR: 12g

DON'T GET BOGGED DOWN BY OUNCES

Don't fret when shopping for the cans in this recipe. If you can find only a 15-ounce can of fire-roasted tomatoes instead of a 14.5-ounce can, don't worry about it. And the same goes for the remaining ingredients. This soup recipe is so forgiving and will be equally as delicious in the end.

Ravioli Lasagna

Did you ever think you could create a perfectly layered lasagna in 15 minutes or less? While these instructions use cheese ravioli, any type of ravioli will work with this extremely easy dish, and you can sub in your favorite. Layer the ingredients and let your Instant Pot® do the rest...genius! And the fresh basil leaves? Well, they aren't necessary, but they sure are delicious.

Pantry Staples: none
Hands-On Time: 15 minutes
Cook Time: 20 minutes

Serves 4

1 (20-ounce) jar marinara sauce
1 (25-ounce) package fresh or frozen cheese ravioli
1 cup grated mozzarella cheese
½ cup grated vegetarian Parmesan cheese
2 cups water
¼ cup fresh basil chiffonade

1 Grease a 7" springform pan. Add ⅓ of marinara sauce to bottom of pan. Add half of ravioli in an even layer(s). Layer ⅓ of marinara sauce over ravioli. Add ½ cup mozzarella cheese in an even layer. Sprinkle with ¼ cup Parmesan cheese. Add remaining ravioli. Pour remaining sauce over ravioli. Add remaining mozzarella and Parmesan cheese.

2 Place a square of aluminum foil along the outside bottom of the pan and crimp up around the edges.

3 Add water to the Instant Pot® and insert steam rack. Place pan on steam rack. Lock lid.

4 Press the Manual or Pressure Cook button and adjust time to 20 minutes. When timer beeps, let pressure release naturally for 10 minutes. Quick-release any additional pressure until float valve drops. Unlock lid.

5 Remove pan from pot. Carefully pour off any water/steam from top of lasagna. Place on a cooling rack for 30 minutes before removing sides of springform pan.

6 Slice and garnish with basil. Serve warm.

PER SERVING:

CALORIES: 742 | FAT: 35g | PROTEIN: 33g | SODIUM: 1,860mg | FIBER: 8g | CARBOHYDRATES: 64g | NET CARBS: 56g | SUGAR: 20g

Red Wine and Mushroom Risotto

Risotto just on its own screams opulence; add red wine and mushrooms—wow! This dish is set to impress.

Pantry Staples: olive oil, vegetable broth, salt, ground black pepper
Hands-On Time: 5 minutes
Cook Time: 19 minutes

Serves 4

- 2 tablespoons olive oil
- 1 small yellow onion, peeled and finely diced
- 1 cup sliced baby bella mushrooms
- 2 cloves garlic, peeled and minced
- 1½ cups Arborio rice
- 3 cups vegetable broth, divided
- 1 cup dry red wine (cabernet sauvignon or pinot noir)
- ½ teaspoon salt
- ¼ teaspoon ground black pepper

1 Press the Sauté button on the Instant Pot® and heat oil. Add onion and mushrooms and stir-fry 3–5 minutes until onions are translucent. Add garlic and rice and cook an additional 1 minute. Add 1 cup broth and stir 2–3 minutes until it is absorbed by rice.

2 Add remaining 2 cups broth, wine, salt, and pepper. Press the Cancel button. Lock lid.

3 Press the Manual or Pressure Cook button and adjust time to 10 minutes. When timer beeps, let pressure release naturally for 10 minutes. Quick-release any additional pressure until float valve drops. Unlock lid.

4 Ladle into bowls. Serve warm.

PER SERVING:

CALORIES: 371 | **FAT:** 7g | **PROTEIN:** 7g | **SODIUM:** 986mg | **FIBER:** 3g | **CARBOHYDRATES:** 64g | **NET CARBS:** 61g | **SUGAR:** 2g

Butter Parmesan Zoodles

If you don't own a spiralizer you can use a vegetable peeler and make long ribbons. Or you can find "zoodled" zucchini fresh in the produce section or even in the frozen vegetable aisle.

Pantry Staples: salt, ground black pepper
Hands-On Time: 10 minutes
Cook Time: 4 minutes

Serves 2

- 3 tablespoons unsalted butter, divided
- 4 medium zucchini, spiraled into "zoodles"
- ¼ cup grated vegetarian Parmesan cheese
- ¼ teaspoon salt
- ¼ teaspoon ground black pepper
- ¼ cup chopped fresh parsley

1 Press the Sauté button on the Instant Pot®. Add 2 tablespoons butter and heat until melted. Add "zoodles" and toss 3–4 minutes until softened.

2 Add remaining butter, cheese, salt, and pepper and toss in pot until butter is melted.

3 Transfer to bowls and garnish with parsley. Serve warm.

PER SERVING:

CALORIES: 274 | FAT: 20g | PROTEIN: 9g | SODIUM: 553mg | FIBER: 4g | CARBOHYDRATES: 15g | NET CARBS: 11g | SUGAR: 10g

Desserts

If you're like most people, you probably have a sweet tooth that pulls at your stomach from time to time. And sometimes you don't want an entire two-layer cake in the house...because you'll just eat it! The great thing about the Instant Pot® is that it creates desserts that are just the right size to make your sweet tooth *and* your scale happy. Most of these desserts provide only 4–6 servings, so you won't be tempted to overeat, and you won't have desserts hanging around your kitchen for days on end. And with dishes ranging from Late Night Brownies and Root Beer Float Cupcakes to Individual Cheesecakes and Peanut Butter Custards, these perfect little delights are guaranteed to hit the spot no matter what you find yourself craving.

Strawberry Upside-Down Cake

Upside-down cakes are not only for pineapples! This sweet twist is a summer dream dessert, especially after a day of strawberry picking at your local farm. Add a scoop of vanilla ice cream next to a slice for an extra-special treat!

Pantry Staples: all-purpose flour, granulated sugar, vanilla extract, baking powder, baking soda, salt
Hands-On Time: 5 minutes
Cook Time: 35 minutes

Serves 4

- 2 cups diced strawberries
- 1 cup plus 1 tablespoon all-purpose flour, divided
- ⅓ cup plus 1 tablespoon granulated sugar, divided
- 1 large egg
- 2 tablespoons unsalted butter, melted
- 1 teaspoon vanilla extract
- 1 cup ricotta cheese
- 2 teaspoons baking powder
- 1 teaspoon baking soda
- ⅛ teaspoon salt
- 1½ cups water

1 Grease a 6″ cake pan. Place a circle of parchment paper in the bottom.

2 In a medium bowl, toss strawberries in 1 tablespoon flour and 1 tablespoon sugar. Add strawberries to pan in an even layer.

3 In a medium bowl, beat egg. Whisk in butter, ⅓ cup sugar, and vanilla until smooth. Add remaining ingredients, including remaining flour, except water. Pour batter into pan over strawberry layer.

4 Add water to the Instant Pot® and insert steam rack. Lower cake pan onto steam rack. Lock lid.

5 Press the Manual or Pressure Cook button and adjust time to 35 minutes. When timer beeps, quick-release pressure until float valve drops. Unlock lid.

6 Remove cake pan from pot and transfer to a cooling rack to cool for 30 minutes. Flip cake onto a serving platter. Remove parchment paper. Slice and serve.

PER SERVING:

CALORIES: 404 | FAT: 14g | PROTEIN: 13g | SODIUM: 702mg | FIBER: 3g | CARBOHYDRATES: 54g | NET CARBS: 51g | SUGAR: 24g

Late Night Brownies

When it's late at night and you are craving a decadent brownie, just make some. You probably have the ingredients lurking in your cabinets. Your sweet tooth can be taken care of with minimal work.

Pantry Staples: vanilla extract, all-purpose flour, granulated sugar, baking powder, baking soda, salt
Hands-On Time: 10 minutes
Cook Time: 25 minutes

Serves 6

2 large eggs, whisked
1 teaspoon vanilla extract
¼ cup all-purpose flour
¼ cup unsweetened cocoa powder
⅓ cup granulated sugar
2 teaspoons baking powder
1 teaspoon baking soda
⅛ teaspoon salt
4 tablespoons unsalted butter, melted
2 tablespoons whole milk
1 cup water
2 tablespoons confectioners' sugar

ADD IT IN!

Change up the flavor of these brownies by adding ⅓ cup of any of the following to the batter before cooking: chopped nuts, different chocolate chip flavors, or chopped dried fruit.

1 Grease a 6″ cake pan.

2 In a large bowl, combine eggs, vanilla, flour, cocoa powder, granulated sugar, baking powder, baking soda, and salt. Stir in butter and milk. Do not overmix. Pour batter into prepared pan.

3 Add water to the Instant Pot® and insert steam rack. Place cake pan on top of steam rack. Lock lid.

4 Press the Manual or Pressure Cook button and adjust time to 25 minutes. When timer beeps, let pressure release naturally for 10 minutes. Quick-release any additional pressure until float valve drops. Unlock lid.

5 Remove cake pan from pot and transfer to a cooling rack to cool 10 minutes.

6 Flip brownies onto a serving platter. Let cool completely 30 minutes. Garnish with confectioners' sugar. Slice and serve.

PER SERVING:

CALORIES: 177 | **FAT:** 9g | **PROTEIN:** 4g | **SODIUM:** 447mg | **FIBER:** 1g | **CARBOHYDRATES:** 21g | **NET CARBS:** 20g | **SUGAR:** 14g

Hot Cocoa Brownies

After a day of snowball fights, how happy would everyone be to eat a Hot Cocoa Brownie while gathered around the fireplace? You'll need only simple ingredients that you probably already have on hand, and everyone will think this was your plan all along!

Pantry Staples: all-purpose flour, granulated sugar, baking powder, baking soda, salt
Hands-On Time: 10 minutes
Cook Time: 25 minutes

Serves 6

2 large eggs, beaten
¼ cup all-purpose flour
2 (1.38-ounce) packets instant hot cocoa mix
⅓ cup granulated sugar
2 teaspoons baking powder
1 teaspoon baking soda
⅛ teaspoon salt
4 tablespoons unsalted butter, melted
⅓ cup mini marshmallows
1 cup water

1 Grease a 6″ cake pan.

2 In a large bowl, combine eggs, flour, hot cocoa mix, sugar, baking powder, baking soda, and salt. Stir in butter and then fold in mini marshmallows. Do not overmix. Pour batter into prepared cake pan.

3 Add water to the Instant Pot® and insert steam rack. Place cake pan on top of steam rack. Lock lid.

4 Press the Manual or Pressure Cook button and adjust time to 25 minutes. When timer beeps, let pressure release naturally for 10 minutes. Quick-release any additional pressure until float valve drops. Unlock lid.

5 Remove cake pan from pot and transfer to a cooling rack to cool 10 minutes.

6 Flip brownies onto a serving platter. Let cool completely 30 minutes. Slice and serve.

PER SERVING:

CALORIES: 214 | **FAT:** 9g | **PROTEIN:** 4g | **SODIUM:** 513mg | **FIBER:** 1g | **CARBOHYDRATES:** 29g | **NET CARBS:** 28g | **SUGAR:** 21g

Stuffed Apples

All of those holiday memories will flood back with the flavors of these Stuffed Apples... especially with a big scoop of vanilla or cinnamon ice cream alongside.

Pantry Staples: vanilla extract, salt
Hands-On Time: 10 minutes
Cook Time: 10 minutes

Serves 4

4 Granny Smith apples
5 tablespoons unsalted butter, softened
2 teaspoons ground cinnamon
¼ cup packed light brown sugar
¼ teaspoon vanilla extract
¼ cup chopped walnuts
⅛ teaspoon salt
2 cups water

ADD IT IN!

Reduce the amount of walnuts to 2 tablespoons and add 2 tablespoons of raisins. Or, if you are avoiding nuts altogether, substitute the full ¼ cup of walnuts for raisins or any dried fruit you enjoy!

1   Core apples, leaving some skin on bottom of hole to hold filling in place. Using a paring knife, remove just a little more of the apple center for a bigger area to fill.

2   In a medium bowl, combine butter, cinnamon, brown sugar, vanilla, walnuts, and salt. Stuff apples with this mixture. Place apples in a 7-cup baking dish.

3   Add water to the Instant Pot® and insert steam rack. Place baking dish on steam rack.

4   Press the Manual or Pressure Cook button and adjust time to 10 minutes. When timer beeps, quick-release pressure until float valve drops. Unlock lid.

5   Allow apples to cool in pot 20 minutes. Serve warm.

PER SERVING:

CALORIES: 327 | FAT: 18g | PROTEIN: 2g | SODIUM: 79mg | FIBER: 6g | CARBOHYDRATES: 39g | NET CARBS: 33g | SUGAR: 30g

Chocolate Cherry Soda Pop Cupcakes

There are a lot of tales as to how exactly soda pop started being added to cakes, one being that wartime sugar was rationed and this was an easy way to sweeten a dessert. It would also cut down on the cooking process because of the innate carbonated personality of soda. But, whatever the legend, try it, and try all the combinations you can imagine, as there are too many to count. Psst...it even works with diet sodas!

Pantry Staples: vanilla extract, salt
Hands-On Time: 10 minutes
Cook Time: 18 minutes

Serves 12

Cupcakes
½ (15.5-ounce) box moist chocolate cake mix
6 ounces (½ can) cherry soda
2 cups water

Chocolate Icing
4 ounces cream cheese, softened
¼ cup unsweetened cocoa powder
4 tablespoons unsalted butter, softened
½ teaspoon vanilla extract
⅛ teaspoon salt
2 cups confectioners' sugar

1 Grease twelve silicone cupcake liners.

2 In a medium bowl, combine cake mix and cherry soda. Spoon mixture into prepared cupcake liners.

3 Add water to the Instant Pot® and insert steam rack. Place six cupcake liners on steam rack. Lock lid.

4 Press the Manual or Pressure Cook button and adjust time to 9 minutes. When timer beeps, quick-release pressure until float valve drops. Unlock lid. Transfer cupcakes to a cooling rack. Repeat cooking process with remaining six cupcake liners.

5 In a medium mixing bowl, cream together cream cheese, cocoa powder, butter, vanilla, and salt. Blend in sugar until smooth. If icing is too loose, add a little more sugar. If icing is too thick, add a little milk.

6 Let cupcakes cool for at least 30 minutes until they reach room temperature, then spread icing on cooled cupcakes. Serve.

PER SERVING:

CALORIES: 212 | **FAT:** 8g | **PROTEIN:** 2g | **SODIUM:** 200mg | **FIBER:** 1g | **CARBOHYDRATES:** 34g | **NET CARBS:** 33g | **SUGAR:** 25g

Root Beer Float Cupcakes

This root beer cake with its vanilla buttercream mimics that classic float. With the first bite, you'll be transformed back to the '50s sitting in front of a soda jerk while swaying to doo-wop playing on the jukebox!

Pantry Staples: vanilla extract
Hands-On Time: 10 minutes
Cook Time: 18 minutes

Serves 12

Cupcakes

½ (15.5-ounce) box moist vanilla cake mix

6 ounces (½ can) root beer

2 cups water

Vanilla Buttercream

1 cup confectioners' sugar

⅓ cup unsalted butter, softened

½ teaspoon vanilla extract

1 tablespoon whole milk

SWAP OUT THAT ROOT BEER!

Are you more of a cola float kind of person? Use a cola instead of root beer. And if you prefer an orange Creamsicle, an orange soda can be substituted. The possibilities are nearly endless!

1 Grease twelve silicone cupcake liners.

2 In a medium bowl, combine cake mix and root beer. Spoon mixture into cupcake liners.

3 Add water to the Instant Pot® and insert steam rack. Place six cupcake liners on steam rack. Lock lid.

4 Press the Manual or Pressure Cook button and adjust time to 9 minutes. When timer beeps, quick-release pressure until float valve drops. Unlock lid. Transfer cupcakes to a cooling rack. Repeat cooking process with remaining six cupcake liners.

5 To make buttercream, cream together vanilla buttercream ingredients in a medium mixing bowl. If buttercream is too loose, add a little more confectioners' sugar. If buttercream is too thick, add a little more milk.

6 Let cupcakes cool for at least 30 minutes until they reach room temperature, then spread buttercream on cooled cupcakes. Serve.

PER SERVING:

CALORIES: 162 | FAT: 6g | PROTEIN: 1g | SODIUM: 124mg | FIBER: 0g | CARBOHYDRATES: 25g | NET CARBS: 25g | SUGAR: 19g

Peachy Crisp

This no-fuss dessert is a great way to use that fresh fruit after a day of peach picking. You probably have many of the other ingredients already in your pantry ready to bring you a comfort dessert. And make sure you have vanilla ice cream in the freezer, because the combination is magical!

Pantry Staples: all-purpose flour, granulated sugar, salt
Hands-On Time: 15 minutes
Cook Time: 12 minutes

Serves 4

3 cups peeled, pitted, and diced peaches
4 tablespoons unsalted butter, melted
½ cup old-fashioned oats
⅛ cup all-purpose flour
¼ cup chopped almonds
⅓ cup granulated sugar
¼ teaspoon ground allspice
¼ teaspoon salt
1 cup water

1 Place peaches in a 7-cup glass baking dish.

2 In a food processor, pulse together butter, oats, flour, almonds, sugar, allspice, and salt until butter is well distributed.

3 Preheat oven to broiler at 500°F.

4 Add water to the Instant Pot® and insert steam rack. Lower glass baking dish onto steam rack. Lock lid.

5 Press the Manual or Pressure Cook button and adjust time to 8 minutes. When timer beeps, let pressure release naturally until float valve drops. Unlock lid.

6 Place dish under broiler 3–4 minutes until browned.

7 Serve warm or chilled.

PER SERVING:

CALORIES: 302 | FAT: 15g | PROTEIN: 4g | SODIUM: 147mg | FIBER: 4g | CARBOHYDRATES: 39g | NET CARBS: 35g | SUGAR: 27g

Banana Bread Pudding

This traditionally rich and luscious dessert is made even better by adding slices of sweet banana. Delicious served after dinner, this bread pudding would also be an excellent choice as a brunch menu item.

Pantry Staples: granulated sugar, salt
Hands-On Time: 10 minutes
Cook Time: 20 minutes

Serves 4

4 cups cubed French bread, dried out overnight

2 small bananas, peeled and sliced

¼ cup granulated sugar

2 cups whole milk

3 large eggs

⅛ teaspoon salt

3 tablespoons unsalted butter, cut into 4 pats

1½ cups water

1 Grease a 7-cup glass baking dish. Add bread, then banana slices. Sprinkle sugar evenly over bananas. Set aside.

2 In a small bowl, whisk together milk, eggs, and salt. Pour over ingredients in glass baking dish and place butter pats on top.

3 Add water to the Instant Pot® and insert steam rack. Place glass baking dish on top of steam rack. Lock lid.

4 Press the Manual or Pressure Cook button and adjust time to 20 minutes. When timer beeps, quick-release pressure until float valve drops. Unlock lid.

5 Remove glass bowl from pot. Transfer to a cooling rack for 30 minutes until set. Serve.

PER SERVING:

CALORIES: 397 | FAT: 16g | PROTEIN: 13g | SODIUM: 401mg | FIBER: 2g | CARBOHYDRATES: 49g | NET CARBS: 47g | SUGAR: 27g

After-Dinner Boozy Hot Cocoa

Sometimes you just want to drink your dessert! Although this recipe calls for Irish cream, don't hesitate to add your favorite liqueur to this drink. And if you have some whipped cream hanging around, invite it to join the cocoa party.

Pantry Staples: granulated sugar, salt, vanilla extract

Hands-On Time: 5 minutes
Cook Time: 5 minutes

Serves 4

6 cups whole milk
¼ cup unsweetened cocoa powder
¼ cup mini chocolate chips
¼ cup granulated sugar
½ cup Irish cream
⅛ teaspoon salt
2 teaspoons vanilla extract

1 Place all ingredients in the Instant Pot®. Lock lid.

2 Press the Steam button and adjust time to 5 minutes. When timer beeps, quick-release pressure until float valve drops. Unlock lid. Whisk ingredients to ensure smoothness.

3 Ladle cocoa into four mugs. Serve warm.

PER SERVING:

CALORIES: 404 | FAT: 14g | PROTEIN: 13g | SODIUM: 240mg | FIBER: 2g | CARBOHYDRATES: 48g | NET CARBS: 46g | SUGAR: 43g

Rice Pudding

Rich and creamy, rice pudding is pure comfort. The extra starch from Arborio rice lends that extra creaminess and softness that other grains just can't provide.

Pantry Staples: vanilla extract, granulated sugar
Hands-On Time: 5 minutes
Cook Time: 25 minutes

Serves 4

1 cup Arborio rice
1½ cups water
1 tablespoon vanilla extract
1 cinnamon stick
1 tablespoon unsalted butter
1 cup golden raisins
¼ cup granulated sugar
½ cup heavy cream

1 Add rice, water, vanilla, cinnamon stick, and butter to the Instant Pot®. Lock lid.

2 Press the Manual or Pressure Cook button and adjust time to 20 minutes. When timer beeps, let pressure release naturally for 10 minutes. Quick-release any additional pressure until float valve drops. Press the Cancel button. Unlock lid.

3 Remove cinnamon stick and discard. Stir in raisins, sugar, and heavy cream.

4 Press the Sauté button on the Instant Pot®, press Adjust button to change temperature to Less, and simmer unlidded 5 minutes. Serve warm.

PER SERVING:

CALORIES: 488 | **FAT:** 13g | **PROTEIN:** 5g | **SODIUM:** 17mg | **FIBER:** 3g | **CARBOHYDRATES:** 86g | **NET CARBS:** 83g | **SUGAR:** 38g

Individual Cheesecakes

These cheesecakes provide the perfect base for whatever fruit is in season or whatever you are craving. Top with fresh berries, ripe peaches, nuts, or even a chocolate drizzle and fresh whipped cream!

Pantry Staples: granulated sugar, salt, vanilla extract
Hands-On Time: 5 minutes
Cook Time: 20 minutes

Serves 6

Crust
18 gingersnaps
3 tablespoons granulated sugar
3 tablespoons unsalted butter, melted
⅛ teaspoon salt

Cheesecake Filling
8 ounces cream cheese, cubed and softened
¼ teaspoon vanilla extract
¼ cup granulated sugar
⅛ teaspoon salt
1 large egg, room temperature
1 cup water

1 Grease six silicone cupcake liners.

2 In a small food processor, pulse together crust ingredients. Transfer crumb mixture to liners and press down along bottom and one-third of the way up sides of liners.

3 With a hand blender or food processor, cream together cream cheese, vanilla, sugar, and salt. Pulse until smooth. Slowly add egg. Pulse 10 seconds. Scrape bowl and pulse until mixture is smooth.

4 Pour mixture into prepared cupcake liners.

5 Add water to the Instant Pot®. Insert steam rack. Place steamer basket on steam rack. Carefully place cupcake liners in basket. Lock lid.

6 Press the Manual or Pressure Cook button and adjust time to 20 minutes. When timer beeps, quick-release pressure until float valve drops. Unlock lid.

7 Remove basket from pot. Let cheesecakes cool at room temperature 10 minutes.

8 Cheesecakes will be a little jiggly in the center. Refrigerate at least 1 hour or up to overnight to allow them to set. Serve chilled.

PER SERVING:

CALORIES: 332 | FAT: 20g | PROTEIN: 4g | SODIUM: 344mg | FIBER: 0g | CARBOHYDRATES: 30g | NET CARBS: 30g | SUGAR: 21g

Chocolate Chip Cheesecake

Are you craving chocolate? Well, get your sweet tooth ready because this dish has a chocolate wafer crust with a smooth creamy filling with chocolate chips—delicious and decadent!

Pantry Staples: granulated sugar, salt
Hands-On Time: 10 minutes
Cook Time: 30 minutes

Serves 6

Crust
22 chocolate wafer cookies
4 tablespoons unsalted butter, melted
Cheesecake Filling
14 ounces cream cheese, cubed and softened
½ cup granulated sugar
⅛ teaspoon salt
2 large eggs, room temperature
½ cup mini semisweet chocolate chips
1 cup water

1 Grease a 7" springform pan and set aside.

2 Add chocolate wafers to a food processor and pulse to combine. Add in butter. Pulse to blend. Transfer crumb mixture to prepared springform pan and press down along the bottom and about ⅓ of the way up sides of pan. Place a square of aluminum foil along the outside bottom of pan and crimp up around edges.

3 With a hand blender or food processor, cream together cream cheese, sugar, and salt. Pulse until smooth. Slowly add eggs. Pulse another 10 seconds. Scrape bowl and pulse until batter is smooth. Fold in chocolate chips.

4 Pour mixture over crust in springform pan.

5 Add water to the Instant Pot® and insert steam rack. Set springform pan on steam rack. Lock lid.

6 Press the Manual or Pressure Cook button and adjust time to 30 minutes. When timer beeps, quick-release pressure until float valve drops. Unlock lid.

7 Lift pan out of pot. Let cool at room temperature 10 minutes. The cheesecake will be a little jiggly in the center. Refrigerate a minimum of 2 hours or up to overnight to allow it to set. Release sides of pan and serve.

PER SERVING:

CALORIES: 520 | FAT: 34g | PROTEIN: 8g | SODIUM: 380mg | FIBER: 1g | CARBOHYDRATES: 38g | NET CARBS: 37g | SUGAR: 30g

Simple Lemon Cheesecake

This luscious and tart creation can be made in less than an hour. The sweet creaminess of the cheesecake against the crunchy cookie crust will have your guests coming back for more.

Pantry Staples: granulated sugar, salt
Hands-On Time: 10 minutes
Cook Time: 30 minutes

Serves 6

Crust
22 vanilla wafer cookies
4 tablespoons unsalted butter, melted

Cheesecake Filling
14 ounces cream cheese, cubed and softened
½ cup granulated sugar
⅛ teaspoon salt
Juice and zest of 1 large lemon
2 large eggs, room temperature
1 cup water

1 Grease a 7″ springform pan and set aside.

2 Add vanilla wafers to a food processor and pulse to combine. Add butter. Pulse to blend. Transfer crumb mixture to prepared springform pan and press down along the bottom and about ⅓ of the way up sides of pan. Place a square of aluminum foil along the outside bottom of pan and crimp up around edges.

3 With a hand blender or food processor, cream together cream cheese, sugar, salt, lemon juice and zest. Pulse until smooth. Slowly add eggs. Pulse another 10 seconds. Scrape bowl and pulse until mixture is smooth.

4 Pour mixture over crust in springform pan.

5 Add water to the Instant Pot® and insert steam rack. Set springform pan on steam rack. Lock lid.

6 Press the Manual or Pressure Cook button and adjust time to 30 minutes. When timer beeps, quick-release pressure until float valve drops. Unlock lid.

7 Lift pan out of pot. Let cool at room temperature 10 minutes. The cheesecake will be a little jiggly in the center. Refrigerate a minimum of 2 hours or up to overnight to allow it to set. Release sides of pan and serve.

PER SERVING:

CALORIES: 447 | FAT: 30g | PROTEIN: 7g | SODIUM: 369mg | FIBER: 0g | CARBOHYDRATES: 30g | NET CARBS: 30g | SUGAR: 23g

Chocolate Mint Chip Pots de Crème

It is so amazing how simple ingredients like eggs, sugar, and cream can create such pure delight. It's even more amazing that the Instant Pot® is a cooking vessel that is able to perfectly steam this custard to perfection.

Pantry Staples: granulated sugar, salt, vanilla extract
Hands-On Time: 15 minutes
Cook Time: 18 minutes

Serves 4

4 large egg yolks
2 tablespoons granulated sugar
⅛ teaspoon salt
¼ teaspoon vanilla extract
1½ cups heavy whipping cream
¾ cups mint chocolate chips
2 cups water

1 In a small bowl, whisk together egg yolks, sugar, salt, and vanilla. Set aside.

2 In a small saucepan over medium-low heat, heat whipping cream to a low simmer, about 2 minutes. Take out a spoonful and whisk it into egg mixture in bowl to temper eggs. Then slowly whisk egg mixture into saucepan with remaining whipping cream.

3 Add mint chocolate chips and continually stir on simmer until chocolate is melted, about 8–10 minutes. Remove from heat and evenly distribute mixture among four custard ramekins.

4 Add water to the Instant Pot® and insert steam rack. Place steamer basket on steam rack. Place ramekins into basket. Lock lid.

5 Press the Manual or Pressure Cook button and adjust time to 6 minutes. When timer beeps, let pressure release naturally for 10 minutes. Quick-release any additional pressure until float valve drops. Unlock lid.

6 Transfer ramekins to a plate and refrigerate covered at least 2 hours or up to overnight. Serve chilled.

PER SERVING:

CALORIES: 550 | **FAT:** 45g | **PROTEIN:** 6g | **SODIUM:** 118mg | **FIBER:** 2g | **CARBOHYDRATES:** 32g | **NET CARBS:** 31g | **SUGAR:** 27g

Peanut Butter Custards

Rich and creamy, this is a must-make for those peanut butter addicts in your house. And if they really want a rush, drizzle a little chocolate sauce over the custards and garnish with some peanut bits before serving.

Pantry Staples: granulated sugar, salt, vanilla extract
Hands-On Time: 15 minutes
Cook Time: 18 minutes

Serves 4

- 4 large egg yolks
- 2 tablespoons granulated sugar
- ⅛ teaspoon salt
- ¼ teaspoon vanilla extract
- 1½ cups heavy whipping cream
- ¾ cup peanut butter chips
- 2 cups water

1 In a small bowl, whisk together egg yolks, sugar, salt, and vanilla. Set aside.

2 In a small saucepan over medium-low heat, heat cream to a low simmer, about 2 minutes. Whisk a spoonful of warm cream mixture into egg mixture to temper eggs. Then slowly add egg mixture back into saucepan with remaining cream.

3 Add peanut butter chips and continually stir on simmer until chips are melted, about 8–10 minutes. Remove from heat and evenly distribute mixture among four custard ramekins.

4 Add water to the Instant Pot® and insert steam rack. Place steamer basket on steam rack. Place ramekins into basket. Lock lid.

5 Press the Manual or Pressure Cook button and adjust time to 6 minutes. When timer beeps, let pressure release naturally for 10 minutes. Quick-release any additional pressure until float valve drops. Unlock lid.

6 Transfer ramekins to a plate and refrigerate covered at least 2 hours or up to overnight. Serve chilled.

PER SERVING:

CALORIES: 627 | FAT: 49g | PROTEIN: 14g | SODIUM: 204mg | FIBER: 1g | CARBOHYDRATES: 33g | NET CARBS: 32g | SUGAR: 27g

Blueberry-Orange Quick Jam

This jam is easy to make, and you don't need canning abilities or pectin. This can be refrigerated up to 3 weeks, if it lasts that long. Spread it on bread, top off your cheesecake, or place a dollop on your morning oatmeal. There are so many ways to enjoy this treat.

Pantry Staples: granulated sugar, salt
Hands-On Time: 10 minutes
Cook Time: 7 minutes

Serves 4

1 pound fresh blueberries
1 cup granulated sugar
Juice and zest from ½ medium orange
⅛ teaspoon salt
½ cup water, divided
2 tablespoons cornstarch

1 Add blueberries, sugar, orange juice and zest, salt, and ¼ cup water to the Instant Pot®. Lock lid.

2 Press the Manual or Pressure Cook button and adjust time to 4 minutes. When timer beeps, let pressure release naturally for 10 minutes. Quick-release any additional pressure until float valve drops. Press the Cancel button. Unlock lid.

3 Create a slurry by whisking together remaining ¼ cup water and cornstarch.

4 Add slurry to berry mixture to thicken, smooshing blueberries against sides of pot as you stir.

5 Press the Sauté button on the Instant Pot® and cook an additional 3 minutes. Allow mixture to cool for at least 30 minutes until it reaches room temperature.

6 Transfer jam to an airtight container and refrigerate until ready to eat. Serve warmed or chilled.

PER SERVING:

CALORIES: 227 | FAT: 0g | PROTEIN: 1g | SODIUM: 74mg | FIBER: 3g | CARBOHYDRATES: 71g | NET CARBS: 68g | SUGAR: 62g

Cinnamon Applesauce

This sentimental dessert will warm your heart. You can also make pork chops the next day and serve some applesauce on the side, as they make a perfect pairing.

Pantry Staples: granulated sugar, salt
Hands-On Time: 20 minutes
Cook Time: 8 minutes

Serves 8

3 pounds apples (any variety), cored and chopped
1 teaspoon ground cinnamon
½ teaspoon ground allspice
½ cup granulated sugar
⅛ teaspoon salt
½ cup freshly squeezed orange juice
⅓ cup water

1 Place all ingredients in the Instant Pot®.

2 Press the Manual or Pressure Cook button and adjust time to 8 minutes. When timer beeps, quick-release pressure until float valve drops. Unlock lid.

3 Use an immersion blender to blend ingredients in pot until desired consistency is reached. Serve warm or cold.

PER SERVING:

CALORIES: 135 | FAT: 0g | PROTEIN: 1g | SODIUM: 38mg | FIBER: 4g | CARBOHYDRATES: 36g | NET CARBS: 32g | SUGAR: 30g

US/Metric Conversion Chart

VOLUME CONVERSIONS

US Volume Measure	Metric Equivalent
⅛ teaspoon	0.5 milliliter
¼ teaspoon	1 milliliter
½ teaspoon	2 milliliters
1 teaspoon	5 milliliters
½ tablespoon	7 milliliters
1 tablespoon (3 teaspoons)	15 milliliters
2 tablespoons (1 fluid ounce)	30 milliliters
¼ cup (4 tablespoons)	60 milliliters
⅓ cup	90 milliliters
½ cup (4 fluid ounces)	125 milliliters
⅔ cup	160 milliliters
¾ cup (6 fluid ounces)	180 milliliters
1 cup (16 tablespoons)	250 milliliters
1 pint (2 cups)	500 milliliters
1 quart (4 cups)	1 liter (about)

WEIGHT CONVERSIONS

US Weight Measure	Metric Equivalent
½ ounce	15 grams
1 ounce	30 grams
2 ounces	60 grams
3 ounces	85 grams
¼ pound (4 ounces)	115 grams
½ pound (8 ounces)	225 grams
¾ pound (12 ounces)	340 grams
1 pound (16 ounces)	454 grams

OVEN TEMPERATURE CONVERSIONS

Degrees Fahrenheit	Degrees Celsius
200 degrees F	95 degrees C
250 degrees F	120 degrees C
275 degrees F	135 degrees C
300 degrees F	150 degrees C
325 degrees F	160 degrees C
350 degrees F	180 degrees C
375 degrees F	190 degrees C
400 degrees F	205 degrees C
425 degrees F	220 degrees C
450 degrees F	230 degrees C

BAKING PAN SIZES

American	Metric
8 x 1½ inch round baking pan	20 x 4 cm cake tin
9 x 1½ inch round baking pan	23 x 3.5 cm cake tin
11 x 7 x 1½ inch baking pan	28 x 18 x 4 cm baking tin
13 x 9 x 2 inch baking pan	30 x 20 x 5 cm baking tin
2 quart rectangular baking dish	30 x 20 x 3 cm baking tin
15 x 10 x 2 inch baking pan	30 x 25 x 2 cm baking tin (Swiss roll tin)
9 inch pie plate	22 x 4 or 23 x 4 cm pie plate
7 or 8 inch springform pan	18 or 20 cm springform or loose bottom cake tin
9 x 5 x 3 inch loaf pan	23 x 13 x 7 cm or 2 lb narrow loaf or pâté tin
1½ quart casserole	1.5 liter casserole
2 quart casserole	2 liter casserole

Index

Note: Page numbers in **bold** indicate recipe category overviews and lists.

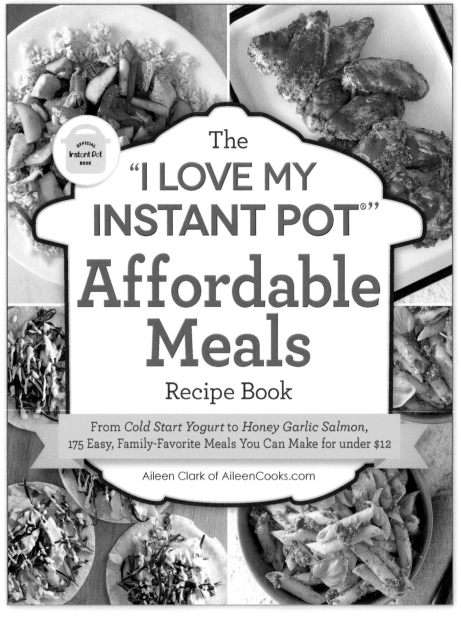